MW00715049

RED LIGHT NEON

RED LIGHT
NEON

A HISTORY OF VANCOUVER'S SEX TRADE

DANIEL FRANCIS

SUB
WAY

VANCOUVER

Copyright © 2006 by Daniel Francis

Library and Archives Canada Cataloguing in Publication

Francis, Daniel
  Red light neon: a history of Vancouver's sex trade/Daniel Francis.

Includes index.
ISBN 0-9736675-2-4

  1. Prostitution--British Columbia--Vancouver--History. I. Title.
HQ150.V3F73 2006   306.74'20971133   C2006-905643-9

Subway Books Ltd.
1819 Pendrell Street, Unit 203
Vancouver, BC V6G 1T3 Canada
Website: *www.subwaybooks.com*
E-mail: *subway@interlog.com*

Design and production: Jen Hamilton

Canadian orders:
Customer Order Department
University of Toronto Press Distribution
5201 Dufferin Street
Toronto, Ontario M3H 5T8

US orders:
University of Toronto Press Distribution
2250 Military Road
Tonawanda, New York 14150
Tel: (716) 693-2768
Fax: (716) 692-7479

Toll-free ordering from Canada or the US:
Tel: 1-800-565-9523
Fax: 1-800-221-9985
Email: *utpbooks@utpress.utoronto.ca*

Contents

INTRODUCTION

Given the clandestine nature of the subject, it is no wonder that the history of prostitution is not well acknowledged in Vancouver. No historic plaques denote former brothels, though such buildings exist. No streets are named after famous streetwalkers, no statues raised to honour any of the city's many madams. But if someone asked me to identify a site where tribute might be paid to the story of Vancouver's sex workers, I would choose the corner of Seymour and Nelson and the neon-lit strip club that has been in business there for fifty years. During the 1960s and 1970s, the Penthouse Cabaret was the city's most notorious nightspot, a hangout for show business celebrities, late-night barflies, hoodlums and high-rollers. The establishment was also a revolving door for prostitutes. As long as they paid their "fees", the women were welcome to set up shop at the tables round the bar. Here a working girl made her contacts, negotiated her price and left on the arm of her date, returning an hour or so later to begin all over again. There were other clubs like it, but they avoided the limelight, whereas the Penthouse, and its sartorially challenged owner Joe Philliponi, revelled in it, enjoying a reputation that extended well beyond the city limits. Allan Fotheringham, whose newspaper column was a must-read in those days, gave the club the status of a tourist attraction, "a minor league equivalent of the Eiffel Tower".

The action at the Penthouse came to a sudden halt the day before Christmas, 1975, when the Vancouver police, for reasons never made clear, shut it down. Which is the real reason it deserves to be commemorated. By closing the Penthouse the police precipitated the most tumultuous period in the history of Vancouver prostitution. In retrospect, everyone agreed that the closure was a major mistake. The decision caused an increase in the number of women on the street, which led to the muddled attempts in the 1980s to clean up the West End, and led as well, indirectly, to the tragedy of the Missing Women. One of my police informants, recalling this period, said it was "almost like the Dark Ages settled in over the streets as far as prostitution was concerned". He meant, I believe, that by hassling the women and their customers, police drove the sex trade deeper into the shadows, creating the conditions in which predators could flourish. To be fair, the police did not get much help from local politicians, who catered to the not-in-my-backyard prejudices of neighbourhood groups. If there was a moment when things went sadly wrong with the city's attempt to regulate commercial sex, a good case can be made that it was here, at the Penthouse in 1975.

Inevitably, the case of the Missing Women is the sad conclusion to this story of the sex trade in Vancouver. The disappearance and murder of so many people from a single neighbourhood is unprecedented in Canadian history. It weighs on the community's conscience. At least, it should do so, and an entire community bears responsibility for the fate of some of its most disadvantaged members. As I write this, the trial of Robert (Willie) Pickton for the murder of twenty-six women is in its early phases. I do not know whether he is guilty of the murders of some or all of these women. The court will decide. I do know that the deaths are an important part of the broader story.

All cities are centres of commerce where goods and services are bought and sold; port cities especially so. Since prostitution is a form of commerce, we should not be surprised to find that it has flourished in Canada's Pacific port. My interest in the history of prostitution grew out of a book I wrote about Louis Taylor, Vancouver's longest-serving mayor, who served eight terms off and on between 1910 and 1935.[1] Taylor had a tolerant attitude towards what we now call vice crimes, including prostitution. Nora Hendrix, a black woman who lived in the Downtown Eastside between the wars (and grandmother of the guitarist Jimi Hendrix), credited Taylor in an interview with creating a red light district. "Everybody liked Mayor Taylor 'cause he was one of those kind of plain men, he looked like he was for everybody", she recalled.

> And they had a red-light district, you see? That was what a lot of people liked about Taylor, having this red-light district, because it did help to keep the people, you know, the what-you-m'a-call women was all in this one category. And when the boats come in, when those fellows want to go somewhere for a good time, well they knew where to go. See, they'd go to this street in this neighbour-hood 'cause it was all set for them.[2]

But not everyone appreciated Taylor's tolerance of prostitution. His years in office were dogged by charges that he was in the pocket of the East End underworld. This aspect of Taylor's career made me interested in finding out more about the history of vice in the city.

✳✳✳

Because it is an activity that goes on clandestinely, prostitution offers particular challenges to the historian. Not a great deal can be discovered about the women who made their living in the sex trade, and such information as does exist is often protected by privacy legislation. As a result, most of the early sources for this study come from the police and the press, not from the women themselves. Yet, since the 1970s several academics and government inquiries have conducted studies of the sex trade and part of their work has involved interviewing prostitutes, so that the voices of the women, and to a lesser degree the young men, are not completely absent. In time, such people will speak for themselves. For the moment, I hope that I have managed in some degree to bring their shadowy world out into the light.

I want to emphasize that this is not a book that is only about victims. Of all the responses that the history of prostitution might elicit—shame, embarrassment, anger, outrage—pity is the least useful. There is no question that prostitutes are victimized: by violent customers, pimps, police and the public. In a larger sense, they are sometimes victims of poverty, abuse and addiction. But that is only part of the story. The sex industry is a world filled with stereotypes, from the carefree whore with a heart of gold to the drug-addled hooker on the streets of the Downtown Eastside, and I do not mean for my book to perpetuate another: the downtrodden victim. Behind the stereotypes are the individual women, trying, often successfully, to find a place for themselves in a society that treats them like dirt. In my view, what they need is not pity but sensible public policies that allow them to exit the industry if they wish or to carry on their business in safety if they do not.

Prostitution offers an unusual perspective on the history of the city's politics, social geography, criminal underlife and moral atmosphere. Unhappily, the story does not show Vancouver in a positive light. This book is a history of hypocrisy. The city's political and social leaders consistently have treated prostitutes as pariahs whose presence was tolerated, sometimes exploited, but never approved. All the while, the authorities collected millions of dollars in fines and licence fees from businesses that everyone knows were, and are, fronts for the sex trade.

Sex workers have never lacked for customers. What they have lacked is a secure place to conduct their business. A vast off-street sex trade flourished while police, at the urging of politicians vowing to purify the city, concentrated their attention on the comparatively small number of street prostitutes who worked out in the open. Because they were considered a nuisance, these sex workers were hounded from street to street and neighbourhood to neighbourhood. Laws were adjusted to criminalize their activities; new ways were found to disrupt their business. These efforts salved the conscience of the morally righteous, but each attempt to discourage prostitution simply forced the women to work in increasingly dangerous circumstances. The end result is the rising death toll that we have seen in the past three decades. It is with the historical origins of this sad story that my book begins.

In the course of my research, many people have helped me with information and insights, not least the authors whose books and reports I have relied on. They are listed in the bibliography. As usual, the staff at the City of Vancouver Archives and the Vancouver Public Library have gone out of their way to help me lay my hands on the needed sources. The public should know how important both institutions are to the history of the city. Chris Mathieson at the Vancouver Police Centennial Museum was very helpful in allowing me to look through the museum collection. My publisher, George Fetherling, gets credit for inspiring the project. He was both critical and encouraging throughout. Thanks also to Bill Harkema, Bob Ley, Marika Sandrelli, Peter Trower and Douglas Trousdell. Of course, none of these people is responsible for any of the conclusions drawn or opinions expressed herein, which are entirely my responsibility.

One

WOMEN AT WORK, 1873–1914

Prostitutes have been at work in Vancouver since before the creation of the city. Birdie Stewart, reputed to be Vancouver's first madam, set up shop in a house near the corner of Water Street and Abbott in 1873 (the same year that the first school opened).[1] At the time, the tiny settlement of wooden buildings strung out along the south shore of Burrard Inlet westward of its only employer, Hastings Mill, was known formally as the Township of Granville. Informally, it was Gastown, named for the garrulous saloon keeper John (Gassy Jack) Deighton, renowned for his ability to talk endlessly about any subject. Deighton had arrived from New Westminster six years earlier with his Squamish wife Whahalia and a barrel of whiskey to open the Globe Saloon.

There is a statue of Gassy Jack erected in what has become one of the city's most popular tourist destinations. Much less is known about Birdie Stewart. She must have had a cheeky sense of humour, because she located her brothel two doors away from the home of the Methodist minister (near the present site of the Lamplighter Pub in modern Gastown).[2] Her presence didn't seem to scandalize anyone in the rough-hewn community, and the lone police officer,

Constable Jonathan Miller, allowed her to conduct her business just a short walk from his jail without interference. There were only a couple of hundred residents in the village. One of these, W.H. Gallagher, described the main thoroughfare, Water Street, as little more than "a wagon trail which corkscrewed a sinuous way in and out among the stumps." Most businesses were located on Water, while one block back was Cordova, "the residential street". At the corner of Cordova and Abbott, Gallagher recalled, "was a row of Chinese cabins and some other occupants of ill repute."[3]

The population was diverse. Portuguese Joe Silvey owned another of the saloons, while his countryman Gregorio Fernandez ran the general store.[4] Josephine and Philip Sullivan, African-Americans from California, operated a restaurant and store. George Black, a Scot, kept a pet bear chained outside the door of his butcher shop. Navvy Jack Thomas, who ran the ferry across the inlet, was Welsh; Gassy Jack himself was a Yorkshireman; most of the mill hands were Chinese or belonged to the Squamish First Nation; Jeremiah Rogers, who logged most of Kitsilano, hailed from New Brunswick; Eihu, who lived with his family in what is now Coal Harbour, was a Kanaka from the Hawaiian Islands. In such a polyglot community, Chinook Jargon was more likely than English to be the language of the street, and the brothel. Stewart's clients would have been a mix of mill hands, prospectors and loggers, and sailors from the growing fleet of ships that put in at the mill to take on lumber.

Everything changed in 1885 when the Canadian Pacific Railway announced that Granville would be the Pacific end point of its transnational line. In return for moving the terminus down the inlet from Port Moody, the rail company received a provincial grant of about 6,500 hectares of land encompassing much of what became the downtown core and much of the area south of False Creek to the Fraser River. A new city was incorporated on 6 April 1886 and named Vancouver at the suggestion of the CPR general manager William Van Horne. Ironically, the company that breathed life into Vancouver also contributed to the terminal city's near destruction. On 13 June, two months after incorporation, CPR crews clearing brush north of False Creek watched in horror as a sudden squall of wind blew burning debris into the surrounding undergrowth. Fanned by the wind, the flames swept down on the small huddle of wooden buildings and in a matter of minutes there was nothing left standing in the city's heart. Then, as quickly as it began, the fire died away, just short of the Hastings Mill. By dawn the next day supplies were pouring down the road from New Westminster and the process of rebuilding was well underway.

Since all of Gastown burned, whatever brothels existed did also. One neighbourhood that survived the fire, however, was the so-called Indian Rancherie just east of the Hastings Mill on the waterfront, at the foot of what is now Campbell Avenue. It consisted of a collection of squatters' shacks, largely but not solely home to Aboriginals who had provided a workforce for the mill since it opened in 1865. The city's respectable element considered the rancherie a shameful centre of depravity. Clerics complained that Aboriginal women went there to prostitute themselves, and there were frequent fights and unruliness. In July 1887 the chief of police evicted all the residents after complaints about nuisance behaviour.[5] As importantly, the CPR line ran right through the rancherie, and the railway did not want the squatters so clearly visible to its passengers. Nonetheless some of the residents remained or returned, and it was not until 1896 that the city's medical officer reported the final destruction of the shacks in the interest of public health.

Meanwhile, brothels continued to operate discreetly in the old Gastown area, rebuilt since the fire, satisfying not only the sexual needs of their customers but also the fiscal needs of the city. Periodically, police raided the houses and madams were hauled into court where they duly paid their fines and went back to work. The precedent was established in 1886 when city council asked the police chief, John Stewart, to round up "drunk and disorderly persons", a category that included prostitutes. Among those arrested were Birdie Stewart and some of her "girls". Mayor Malcolm MacLean, acting as magistrate, fined them $20 each.[6] The arrangement benefited the city, which obtained much needed revenue, and was accepted by the brothel keepers as a tax on doing business.

So long as Vancouver (Granville) was a frontier mill town with a floating, mainly male population, authorities tolerated prostitution and saw no need to persecute the women who practised it. Commercial sex provided a public service, fulfilling the needs of the transient males who periodically descended on the city from their jobs in the seasonal logging, mining and construction camps. In *Woodsmen of the West,* his history of coastal logging disguised as a novel, Martin Grainger describes these men during their stay in the city "drifting up the street to the Terminus and down the street to the Eureka, and having a drink with the crowd in the Columbia bar, and standing drinks for the girls at number so-and-so Dupont Street." Some even holed up for the duration in the classier brothels. "I have known men of a romantic disposition who took lodgings in those houses where champagne is kept on the premises and where there is a certain society."[7] As Grainger suggests, saloons and hotel bars were convenient places for prostitutes and customers to make their arrangements. Vancouver was a city that loved its drink. After all, it had originated in the 1860s as a tiny settlement centred around Gassy Jack's Globe Saloon. By 1901, a city of just 27,000 people boasted forty-seven hotels, twelve saloons, seven liquor stores and a variety of illegal "blind pigs". In the province generally, liquor consumption was double the national average. In Vancouver, bars stayed open twenty-four hours a day; whatever Sunday closing laws were on the books were generally ignored.[8]

But while initially laws reflected a tolerant attitude towards commercial sex, the situation changed following Confederation, when the Criminal Code of Canada viewed prostitution as a public order issue and dealt with it under an 1869 law, *An Act Respecting Vagrants*. In the quaint language of the day, this law prohibited "all common prostitutes, or night walkers wandering in the fields, public streets or highways, lanes or places of public meeting or gathering of people, not giving a satisfactory account of themselves." The law also singled out "keepers of bawdy houses and houses of ill-fame" and people "who do for the most part support themselves by the avails of prostitution". All these individuals—prostitutes, madams and pimps— were liable to jail terms of several months and/or fines of up to $50. By the 1890s, federal lawmakers were taking an even dimmer view of prostitution and sexual predation. The historian Constance Backhouse describes "an explosion of legislation" during the last two decades of the nineteenth century aimed at protecting innocent women from being debauched and led into prostitution by pimps and brothel keepers.[9] This trend culminated in 1892 with the stiffening of the sexual predation provisions of the federal Criminal Code. As well, penalties were increased for keeping bawdy houses and for living on the earnings of prostitution. In addition to the federal statutes, there were bylaws passed by local governments aimed at controlling commercial sex. The principal one in Vancouver was an anti-vagrancy bylaw that allowed the prosecution of anyone connected to an "immoral house".

No matter what laws were in place, however, there was not usually much enthusiasm for enforcing them. By 1892, there were reported to be seventeen or eighteen brothels in the city, but the civic police committee was instructing officers to take a permissive attitude towards them as long as the women were circumspect and the public did not have its nose rubbed in their activities. Of course, even if the authorities had wanted to curtail prostitution, there is the question of whether they could have done so, given the size of the force and the limited penal facilities. At its incorporation, Vancouver had a single police officer, John Stewart, assisted by a one-armed jailer who doubled as the lamplighter. By the mid-1890s the force had grown to twelve members, but the city jail consisted of only four cells in the original city hall on Powell Street. When civic officials moved over to a new city hall on Main Street in 1898, there was room for the jail to expand to eight cells, plus the tumbledown hut in the backyard to accommodate women.[10] For the most part, this facility was used as a holding tank for drunks. The new police station that opened in 1904 at the corner of Cordova and Main contained forty cells, still not enough to house the casualties from any "war on vice".

✳ ✳ ✳

The first decade of the twentieth century was a period of tremendous growth in Vancouver. The Klondike gold rush of 1897–98, and the business opportunities it generated, ignited an economic boom that did not sputter out until the eve of the First World War. "The forest vanished and up went the city," observed the novelist Ethel Wilson, who was a young girl living in the West End at the turn of the century.[11] The population quadrupled in ten years; the 1911 census showed that Vancouver had become Canada's fourth-largest city, just behind Winnipeg. The city also grew in area, spreading eastward to Boundary Road and south beyond Sixteenth Avenue. The adjacent communities of South Vancouver and Point Grey added another 20,000 residents.

Transportation keyed Vancouver's emergence as the business capital of the province. The magnificent harbour welcomed vessels from around the world. Ships departed carrying grain from the Prairies, lumber from the coastal forests, and minerals from the booming mines of the Interior. By 1904, two transcontinental rail lines terminated in the city, and the municipal trolley system was growing rapidly. All this growth touched off a construction boom. Anyone with spare cash was investing in real estate. Each year, the value of building permits increased until, in 1912, at the peak of the boom, $20 million worth of new construction was going up. Nothing symbolized commercial expansion so much as the new skyscrapers that were transforming the downtown skyline. Chief among these was the thirteen-storey Dominion Building on Hastings Street; when it was completed in 1910, it was the tallest building in the British Empire. A dozen chartered banks opened for business during this period, as did Charles Woodward's department store, a new Hotel Vancouver and the new provincial courthouse on Georgia Street (now the art gallery). By the end of 1912, Vancouver had eighty kilometres of paved streets and just over three hundred kilometres of concrete sidewalks. The frontier town of dirt streets and wooden buildings had become a modern city.

Like every other business, prostitution flourished during the boom, a fact that disturbed many of Vancouver's respectable citizens. The tolerant, live-and-let-live attitude of an earlier time was replaced by periodic outbreaks of moral fervour. One of these occurred in 1896, when several of the brothels on Dupont Street (as East Pender was known until 1907) at the western edge of Chinatown were burned by the city under the pretext of being in violation of sanitary codes. The majority of the buildings survived this purge, however, and Dupont Street remained Vancouver's red light district for several more years. It was an unpaved street of two-storey clapboard buildings, some with balconies on their upper floors. At high tide, the waters of False Creek, then much larger than it is today, lapped at the foundations of the buildings on the south side of the street. During the day, Dupont Street was a bustle of Chinese vegetable vendors and drovers leading herds of cattle to the slaughterhouse at the other end of town. At night, the red lights winked on and the wooden sidewalks filled with mobs of men in search of drink and companionship. In 1899, an investigation into police practices revealed that constables were accepting bribes, sharing the proceeds of fines and otherwise turning a blind eye to the activities of the prostitutes. As a result, the police chief was fired, then quietly rehired.[12] One madam who apparently lost her police protection was Florence Mackenzie, known as "Mother Mackenzie", a white-haired, sixty-five-year-old keeper of a house at 37 Dupont Street. In August 1899 she was charged with procuring and sentenced to two years in the provincial jail. "This woman has been a prostitute in nearly every city on the continent," reads a note on the record book, "and is one of the worst of her kind."[13]

In the summer of 1903, Mayor Thomas Neelands served notice that the houses on Dupont Street would have to move. "These women certainly have to go," he told the *Daily Province*. "The location of these houses is far too central to be allowed to remain, now that the city is showing such a tendency to grow in that quarter." Progress was closing in on Dupont Street. But where should the ladies go? The mayor refused to speculate, and in the end he was outvoted by his council, which agreed to postpone doing anything about the matter, instead leaving it to the police committee to handle. The majority of councillors recognized that if they forced prostitutes out of one area they would probably move to other even less acceptable neighbourhoods.[14] Nonetheless, early in March the following year, city police raided several houses on Dupont Street as the first step in a campaign to close down the district. The brothel operators fought back. They hired lawyer W.J. Bowser, an influential Conservative and a future premier of the province, to defend them in court, where they were charged under the provisions of the vagrancy bylaw. They chose to put forward Dora Reno, the owner of 140 Dupont Street, commonly known as the White House, as a test case. No one denied that the address in question was a "house of assignation". Instead, "Billy" Bowser challenged the bylaw itself, arguing that it was *ultra vires*; in other words, that the city had no authority to pass the law in the first place. After deliberating for two weeks the police magistrate agreed that the civic bylaw trespassed on the exclusive powers of the federal Parliament and dismissed the charges against Reno and the others.[15] After that, the steam went out of the campaign to close Dupont Street. Not long afterwards, police raided a set of furnished rooms above the Empire Theatre on

East Hastings near the Carnegie Library. "This is the first raid made by the police during recent years on an alleged house of ill-repute outside the restricted district," noted the *Daily Province*. The keeper was Mary Vincent, who had been operating on Dupont Street until her recent move to Hastings. The magistrate fined the three men who were found in the rooms $25 each and remarked, "we must keep these houses within the confines of Dupont Street if we can," making it clear that authorities wanted to maintain the "restricted district".[16]

Who were the women who engaged in prostitution in early Vancouver? A few details of their lives emerge only when they came into contact with the law.[17] Some were very young. Annie Flack, for instance, was a sixteen-year-old girl from Germany who got six months in jail for being a "common streetwalker". Lizzie Cooke, seventeen, was an American seamstress who got three months for soliciting. Some were more experienced, like Julia Lebrun, the forty-year-old keeper of a bawdy house at 130 Dupont who took thirty days in jail instead of paying a $35 fine. Some were thought to be drug addicted, like Grace Cooper, "a hypo fiend of the worst kind" who had a long list of convictions that included bank robbery, vagrancy and street walking. Some were arrested for other crimes. Rosie Garland, a nineteen-year-old prostitute supposedly from Paris, was sentenced to eighteen months for stealing $60 from a man at the Dougal House Hotel. Rita King, a twenty-year-old "sporting woman", went to jail for three years for shooting another prostitute in a jealous rage at the Opera Resort Saloon. Eva Mack, an African-American from the US, was arrested for stealing $18. "This woman got G. Liscomb to go into the alley and while having connections with him she stole his money." The court gave her six hours to leave town, a sentence meted out to many of the American women. The impression gained from such cases is that these were hard-luck women, forced by poverty, racial prejudice and drug dependency into selling themselves in the streets and brothels. Their careers did not last long. Given the state of birth control, unwanted pregnancies were common. Back-alley abortionists and self-administered remedies would have taken their toll in injury and death. Other occupational hazards included venereal disease, drug and alcohol abuse, and the violence of pimps and clients. One reason so many prostitutes were young was that so many did not survive to grow old.

The issue of Dupont Street re-emerged in 1906. A key factor seems to have been the presence of the Vancouver Westminster & Yukon Railway, a subsidiary of the Great Northern, an American line that had arrived from Seattle two years earlier. The VW&Y built its terminus on the south side of Dupont at the corner of Columbia Street and its owners, who were miffed that passengers were disembarking into the heart of the city's vice district, added their considerable influence to the familiar complaints of the moral reformers. Early in June, the police chief, Sam North, announced that he had told the Dupont Street madams "to hunt for new quarters". There was much speculation in the press as to where the women would go. Would they move to Park Lane (since obliterated by the VIA Rail station) on the shores of False Creek on the southern border of Strathcona? Would they disperse to rooming houses along Granville, Hastings and Main streets, upsetting local businesses? The *Daily Province* revealed that "the consensus of opinion is that the women will not be molested if they establish themselves in China town." But the issue was a political hot potato, and both

North and the mayor denied indignantly that they had arranged for a safe haven for the city's brothels. The Moral Reform Association joined the fray, insisting in a letter to city council that "the social evil is one which cannot in any way be sanctioned, being contrary to all laws of decency and morality."[18] In the middle of this debate, Chief North was fired when one of the Dupont Street madams testified in court that she had paid him a bribe to leave her establishment alone.[19] In August, his successor, C.A. Chisholm, announced a vigorous offensive against the brothels. "I think I will move not against the women of the district," he said, "but against the owners of the property in which they are residing. In that way I will get at the parties who are reaping the real benefit of the traffic in high rentals which are being charged in such places." Chief Chisholm, however, recognized what the moral zealots pretended not to: that once he had chased the women out of Dupont Street, they would open for business somewhere else. "I make no concealment of my view," he told a reporter, "that ultimately one place, one district remote from respectable streets and centres, will have to be set aside for these dames. It must come to that with Vancouver, as it has with hundreds of other cities."[20]

Not everyone believed that the police were as successful as they claimed to be in cleaning up Dupont Street. At the end of October, the licence commissioner, William Hunt, paid an evening visit to Vancouver's "tenderloin". (According to historian Timothy Gilfoyle, this term for a city's vice district originated in New York in the 1870s.[21]) Strolling along not two blocks from City Hall, he found the brothels doing a brisk business. Young men loitered on the sidewalks; red lights glowed above the doorways; women in flimsy pink kimonos leaned out of the windows and beckoned to him as he passed. "I think the conditions in the tenderloin have not been so bad for the past four years," he reported. Chief Chisholm could only respond that the women were in the process of leaving the street. In August there had been forty-one brothels occupied by 153 prostitutes, he said; as of October the number of women was down to sixty-four, and early in November the *Province* reported that the last of the Dupont Street houses had closed.[22]

As Chisholm predicted, they did not move very far. Running south off Dupont Street just west of Carrall were two dead-end lanes known as Canton Alley and Shanghai Alley. Until the 1920s, they were the centre of Vancouver's Chinatown. Only a block long, Shanghai Alley, a narrow dirt laneway, bustled with life. Residents occupied tiny rooms in the three-storey tenements and rooming houses. Restaurants and laundries operated on the ground floor, along with the Sing Kew Theatre, a five-hundred-seat space devoted to Chinese opera, theatre and public meetings. Parallel to Shanghai Alley was Canton Alley, more of a long courtyard. A variety of stores were at street level, with apartments crammed into the tenements above. A number of brothels opened in the alleys in the autumn of 1906, and the antagonism towards prostitution became mixed with the anti-Asian sentiment so strong in the city. Chinese residents had been congregating in the vicinity of Dupont and Carrall streets since the early 1890s, choosing to live in close proximity to one another in the face of white hostility and discrimination. Gradually this area emerged as an informal "Chinatown" where most Chinese people lived and carried on their businesses.

By 1901, the district numbered 2,100 residents, about seven percent of the city's total population. The majority were single men, most of whom could not afford to pay the head tax that the government imposed on immigrants from China. As a result, they could not bring their families to Canada. They cleared land, worked in laundries, brickyards, fish canneries, sawmills, and on coastal steamers, or were tailors, household cooks and servants. Despite the value of this workforce to the local economy, anti-Asian racism was the norm among the city's white majority who claimed that Asian immigrants drove down wages and threatened Anglo-Saxon values. Racial antagonism bubbled over into violence in September 1907 when an anti-Asian rally outside City Hall on Main Street got out of control. A mob of protestors marched around the corner into Chinatown where they broke windows and smashed shopfronts. Doubling back to Japantown on Powell Street, the mob was met by residents armed with clubs and bottles, and by the time police and firefighters restored order several thousand dollars' damage had been done to Chinese- and Japanese-owned businesses.

In the white imagination, Chinatown was a place of filth and immorality where young white maidenhood was defiled and inno-cent young males seduced. Three vices in particular were associated with Chinatown. Opium was legal in Canada until 1908, and Chinatown was considered to be riddled with dens where the drug could be purchased and consumed by both Chinese and whites. "Chinamen keep opium dens where our young men are led into contracting this habit," warned the *Daily Province*, "which marks them for utter ruination and pushes them deeper into the mire of immorality."[23] Outsiders also considered the Chinese to be addicted to gambling. Fan-tan, lotteries, chuckaluck and other harmless pas-times for men whose life in the city was constrained by lack of money and the absence of family were portrayed by the white press as depraved and squalid. Much of the exoticism of Chinatown to outsiders involved stories about gambling dens in narrow laneways protected by false doors and elaborate warning systems. The third vice was prostitution.

Within a year of the crackdown on Dupont Street, 105 brothels were operating in Canton Alley and Shanghai Alley. Most of these would have been simple rooms rather than full-fledged houses.[24] Chinese-run brothels imported young women from China but also housed non-Asian women. In November 1906, a flood of American prostitutes washed into Canton Alley. Some of these women would have been refugees from San Francisco, where a devastating earthquake earlier in the year had destroyed much of the city's tenderloin district and caused many of its inhabitants to move north up the coast to Seattle, Victoria and Vancouver. Police raided the alley and thirty-two women appeared in police court. "Garnet and Ruth and Daisy and Myrtle and Della and all the other twenty-seven were Washington and Oregon birds of brightest plumage, who have been partaking of the hospitality of the Canton Street nest for the past two months," reported the *Daily Province*. "Five women keepers were fined $50 and costs; inmates, $35 and costs; piano-players and housekeepers, $25 and costs." The raids, said Chief Chisholm, were a "gentle warning" to the women to go back south of the border. The following March, police raided another of the Canton Alley establishments and arrested Yet Sun, a Hastings Street shoe dealer, who turned out to be the agent for an absentee Chinese landlord. Also charged were an African-American piano player, a Chinese cook and three "Ethiopian boarders". Rosy Rose, the house-keeper, had fled.[25]

One evening a self-appointed delegation of civic officials toured the area with a reporter.

The party first visited Shanghai Alley, which at the time was crowded with boys and young men gathered about the doors of the dens of vice which have recently been located there. A long string of red lights told all too plainly the nature of the resorts, but some of the denizens have gone still farther, and glittering name-signs were displayed. But as though this was not enough, from behind the curtains and through the half-opened doors the women of the street could plainly be seen inviting passers-by to enter. As quickly as visitors to the place left, the occupants of the room attired in the briefest of skirts, and with decollete apparel to the limit, took their choice from the waiting crowd about the door.[26]

The delegation found similar scenes in Canton Alley.

Chinese business leaders petitioned the city to remedy the situation, and police made sporadic raids, but the two alleys, and Chinatown in general, continued to be a centre for prostitution.

A second district that opened following the dispersal from Dupont Street was Shore Street, a short street of rundown buildings running west off Main a few blocks south of Hastings. Thinking that this area might become the unofficial restricted district they had been seeking, authorities told the madams that they would be undisturbed if they kept order in their houses and did not allow the women to troll for customers in theatres or appear on the streets in conspicuous dress. Nonetheless, the new district gave offence. Business owners from Main Street complained that long lines of men crowded the neighbourhood into the small hours of the morning as though they were queuing for a baseball game. In mid-1911, the brothels had to abandon Shore Street as well.[27] Instead, early the next year, they settled into Alexander Street, north of

Powell, closer to the waterfront and to Hastings Mill, still the city's largest employer.

✳ ✳ ✳

Vancouver was not the only Canadian city in the pre-war era struggling to find an appropriate location for prostitutes to carry on their business. One of the most controversial civic initiatives in this regard took place in Winnipeg where an experiment with an officially endorsed red light district sparked a storm of controversy. Vancouver played a small role in the Winnipeg experiment. In November 1910, John Moncreiff, the managing editor of the Winnipeg *Tribune*, wrote to Vancouver's mayor, Louis Taylor, to enquire how the city was dealing with the prostitution issue. Mayor Taylor's secretary wrote back, reviewing the Dupont Street episode and explaining how the brothels had been removed to Shore Street, reporting that the experiment had been a success. "Judging from other cities on the Pacific Coast and their efforts to cope with the evil His Worship thinks this city has the condition well in hand under the present system…"[28] As we know, the Shore Street red light district was not a success and the brothels had to relocate again, but at the time Vancouver seemed to offer a precedent that Winnipeg might emulate.

Along with enormous economic growth, Winnipeg in the first decade of the new century had experienced an increase in prostitution. As the "Gateway to the West", the city welcomed the vast numbers of immigrants who stormed onto the Canadian Prairies in the pre-war period. A disproportionate number of these newcomers were single men, who provided a ready market. As in Vancouver, prostitutes in Winnipeg were herded from place to place at the insistence of civic leaders and under the pressure of urban development. At the same time, church leaders lobbied against the idea of a segregated district. They wanted the prostitutes driven from the city, and from time to time they enjoyed the support of city hall. In 1909, however, a more tolerant administration was in office, one that favoured regulation over abolition. The police commission gave the police chief, John McRae, the task of establishing a formal red light district where prostitution could be concentrated. In consultation with prominent madams, McRae selected Point Douglas, an isolated point of land along the CPR tracks within walking distance of downtown and home to warehouses, a gas plant, a power station, factories and a flour mill. The move was conducted in a manner that one would expect in a city experiencing a land boom: McRae asked a real-estate agent named John Beaman to organize the operation. Beaman bought up more than twenty houses in the neighbourhood, then resold them to the madams at up to four times the market value. (Ever since, the unproven suspicion has been that Beaman was using capital provided by, and sharing profits with, partners who did not want their involvement in the scheme to become public knowledge.[29])

The women were expected to undergo regular medical checkups and ensure that rowdy behaviour was kept to a minimum. In return for not drawing attention to themselves, they were more or less allowed to go about their business, with the exception of the occasional police raid to keep up appearances. As one historian, Alan Artibise, has pointed out, Point Douglas was a highly profitable operation, and not only for the madams. The civic government regularly collected fines as a form of business tax. The liquor trade, including the licensing agencies, made a killing from the sale of booze, both legal and illegal. Even the telephone company profited from the installation of pay phones in the houses. A lot of people had a vested interest in keeping the red light district functioning smoothly and out of the headlines. But that was not to be. The remaining working-class residents of Point Douglas were not happy at having to share their neighbourhood while watching their property values tumble. The area became an attraction for voyeurs titillated at the sight of barely clad women spilling out of doorways and drunken men reeling down the sidewalks, bootleg liquor being the second-most popular commodity for sale in the brothels. Residents were often accosted in the street by drunks looking to get laid. By the summer of 1910, there were fifty brothels open for business and Point Douglas had become, in the words of historian James Gray, "a massive orgiastic obscenity".[30]

At that point, church workers and activists began a public campaign to clean up Point Douglas, a movement energized that November when the Toronto *Globe* carried an interview with Rev. Dr. J.G. Shearer, general secretary of the Moral and Social Reform Council. Shearer, who recently had been in Winnipeg as part of a tour of western Canada, told the *Globe* reporter that it was "the rottenest city in Canada" where the "social evil" was running rampant, openly condoned by civic officials.[31] (It was at this point that the *Tribune* got in touch with Mayor Taylor in Vancouver, wanting to know how prostitution was handled out on the coast.) The members of Winnipeg city council, alarmed at what Shearer's comments were doing to the image of their city and to their chances of success in the upcoming civic election, asked the provincial government to appoint an inquiry into the Point Douglas situation. But while Mr.

Justice Hugh Robson was conducting his hearings, city voters went to the polls and re-elected Mayor Sanford Evans, whose support for the segregated district was a matter of public record. In a sense, voters had rendered Judge Robson's commission irrelevant. When he reported in January 1911 that the red light district in Point Douglas was disturbing the peace of the neighbourhood, lowering property values and corrupting morals, the response was muted. The police stepped up their patrols and a few of the brothels closed, but the segregated district endured.[32]

The brouhaha over the Point Douglas brothels in Winnipeg and the "restricted district" in Vancouver reflected a much wider national, even international, campaign against prostitution or, as it was increasingly characterized, white slavery. The historian John McLaren has called the first two decades of the twentieth century "the greatest period of moral and social unease about prostitution and its exploitative aspects" in Canada's history.[33] Although prostitution and white slavery became synonymous, the latter technically involved the abduction of young women and their forced participation in commercial sex. Often the victims were thought to have been spirited from one country to another, usually by vile "foreigners" with no respect for the sanctity of white womanhood. While there was little evidence that much of this activity was going on, at least in Canada, white slavery became a new way of thinking about prostitution. Along with being a source of danger to men, the prostitute was now in danger herself. She was victim as well as victimizer. Previously prostitutes had been characterized as fallen women, women of loose virtue, immoral seducers. Transformed into the white slave, they became innocent prey in the urban jungle, damsels in distress who needed rescuing from the evil clutches of foreign pimps and traffickers in human flesh. Today this seems the stuff of Victorian melodrama, but around the turn of the twentieth century "white slavery" was the basic trope by which many people understood prostitution.

What might be called the white-slavery panic emerged in England in the 1880s and spread to continental Europe. Soon it had developed into a worldwide campaign to stamp out the traffic in young women and prostitution generally. Several countries signed on to a Convention on the International Suppression of White Slave Traffic. Anti-prostitution laws were tightened. In the United States, Congress passed the notorious Mann Act, which prohibited the transport of females across state lines for immoral purposes, and several major cities conducted investigations of the "social evil", so called because it was considered a threat to the very foundations of a moral society.

In Canada, a coalition of women's groups, militant churches and social reformers stirred up public concern about the dangers of prostitution. In Toronto, city council appointed a commission to investigate the prevalence of vice and the problem of the white slave traffic. The Protestant churches established the Moral and Social Reform Council of Canada to lobby governments to make changes to their vice laws. This purity brigade carried out a nationwide campaign against prostitution and any officials who appeared to tolerate it in their communities. Their efforts bore fruit in 1913 when the federal government made changes to the Criminal Code aimed at stamping out a range of prostitution-related activities, including the procuring of young girls.

In Vancouver, the fight against organized vice was spearheaded by the provincial chapter of the Moral and Social Reform Council, along with the churches, various women's groups, the YM/YWCA and a group of civic activists calling itself the Good Government League. In March 1912, forty delegates from this coalition attended a meeting of the police commission to press their case for a "moral cleaning up of the rooming houses" in Alexander Street, where a new restricted district was getting established. Speaking for the group, Rev. D.C. Pidgeon urged civic officials to adopt a policy of complete suppression of the "social evil". The experience of other cities, he argued, showed that far from containing prostitution, a segregated district served as a breeding ground for vice. Other speakers complained about the effect the existence of places such as Alexander Street had on the morals of young people. A Rev. Kaburagi pointed out that the location of the brothels so near to the city's Japanese community was a disgrace and opposed by every Japanese resident, while George Gibson declared that the Good Government League "stood for no compromises [and was] absolutely against the recognition of the social evil in any shape or form and would fight it to the last breath." In response to this gust of moral fervour, Mayor James Findlay assured the delegation that neither he nor the police commission approved of the goings-on in Alexander Street. But he pointed out a number of mitigating factors, including the welfare of the women involved, the difficulty of making successful prosecutions in the courts and the likelihood that if driven out of one neighbourhood the women would simply move to another. He said that he was committed to "cleaning up the city" but preferred a more methodical, "step by step" approach to a problem "that requires time and careful handling".[34]

Three months after this meeting, the Reform Council published its views on the question of commercialized sex in a pamphlet titled *Social Vice in Vancouver*.[35] The Council had sent "a special committee of professional and businessmen" to tour Alexander Street. These men concluded that the area was a "vice colony" that should not be tolerated. Surrounding homeowners were being harassed and children at the nearby school corrupted; respectable women feared to walk the streets. The council argued against the whole concept of a restricted district. In its view, Alexander Street was attracting "evildoers" from all over, then radiating vice out into the rest of the city. "The so-called restricted area has always been a distributing centre from which the evil spread all over the city and its environs." *Social Vice in Vancouver* demanded a vigorous assault on prostitution. "Surely the time is come resolutely to clean out all vile nests that harbour social vice and degrade human beings for mercenary ends." It took issue with police and civic officials who were attempting to find some part of the city where prostitution might be out of sight, out of mind. "The fact of the matter is that when a community tolerates the vice anywhere it puts a stamp of approval upon it and encourages it everywhere. Whereas a policy of suppression discourages it everywhere."

The local labour movement staked out a position at the opposite end of the spectrum of opinion. In an article headed "Sex Prostitution Rampant, Who And What's To Blame" in the *British Columbia Federationist,* a leading labour newspaper, J.W. Wilkinson excoriated the "smug self-righteousness" of the "Goody Government League type" who objected to a red light district. Wilkinson, who was secretary of the Vancouver Trades and Labour Council, argued that economics lay at the heart of the issue. As long as many young men could not afford to marry, they resorted to prostitutes who, for the most part, were women "who cannot support themselves on the low wages paid to them by employers". Wilkinson argued that prostitution was better localized in one neighbourhood than spread across the city. "While the bodies and souls of women are exploited for profit in the department stores and factories and shops it is not possible for thousands of them to earn enough to preserve their honour and chastity."[36]

Civic officials were closer to Wilkinson's point of view than to the ardent abolitionism of the moral crusaders. As part of a policy to contain prostitution rather than attempt to eradicate it, police periodically raided the Alexander Street brothels and arrested the women found inside. This policy was made clear by Walter Leek, a member of the police commission. "We had in Vancouver when we took office, a restricted area," he told the *Daily Province*. "The police authorities tolerated it because they could see that it was their duty first to stamp out, as much as possible, prostitution in the residential and uptown business districts. To afford protection to our youth by preventing the casual acquaintance with immoral persons that might lead to downfall, was our first duty." Alexander Street was "the least of the evils", Leek went on, and the policy was to control the area, not abolish it.[37] Leek's remarks were greeted with outrage by the moral reformers, but clearly he was enunciating unofficial civic policy.

At the same time, William Bowser, who had become provincial attorney general in Richard McBride's Conservative government, was drawn back into the controversy over prostitution in the city. Bowser had told civic officials that there was not enough room in provincial jails to accommodate large numbers of those convicted on prostitution-related charges. He argued that the large number of women who were recent arrivals from south of the border should be deported and the others fined rather than sent to jail. "I want to know what good it would do to put these women in jail for six months", he asked. "Has anything been accomplished when they get out? If anything, I think they are more vicious against society."[38] The Liberal press responded to Bowser's moderate remarks as though he had suggested giving the keys of the city to the Mafia. "His statement is an announcement to the underworld that they can go to any extremes of vice," fumed the editor of the *Sun*,

> not only in the segregated district, but everywhere else in British Columbia, without fear of being seriously molested. The impulse which this announcement has already given to the commerce of vice is simply stupendous. As the good tidings have gone out to every tenderloin in the lowest purlieus of the American cities, recruits will swarm to the happy hunting ground in British Columbia where the scarlet woman and her souteneur and all the vile degenerates who flourish on the avails of prostitution are promised the protection of the chief law officer of the Crown.[39]

Like the Reform Council, the *Sun* was confident that prostitution could be eradicated by a strict enforcement of the law.

✳ ✳ ✳

In the midst of this controversy, a reporter for the newspaper *The Truth* paid a visit to Alexander Street. His report played to the widely held belief that Vancouver was becoming a West Coast Sodom. It described perfumed women in fancy dress "strewn all over the street" and men in the houses getting drunk on twenty-five-cent glasses of beer and dancing all night to the music of "a rather sunburned lady on the piano". It described the furtive Chinese housekeepers who collected the money and the "hawk-eyed" madams who raked in the profits. In the House of All Nations, the reporter discovered, "you can get everything from a chocolate coloured damsel up to a Swede girl." And there was nothing clandestine about these operations. "All the lights are blazing and the front door is open to all and sundry who have the money to spend..." At some addresses, the names of the madams appeared in mosaic tile on the entranceways' floors. Alexander Street, the article concluded, "was never as open as it is now." [40]

Women operated most brothels of this period and sometimes even owned the houses. In a world that offered them few business opportunities, brothel keeping was an attractive proposition for women with a head for figures and a taste for the nightlife. The historian Linda Eversole has written about Stella Carroll, whose career was typical of a pre-war, high-end madam. [41] Carroll, an American, arrived in Victoria at the end of 1899 on a visit and decided to stay when the opportunity to own a brothel presented itself. Eventually she owned a pair of tastefully furnished parlour houses, one of them on a five-hectare property just outside the city. Carroll charged her girls rent and allowed them to keep their earnings, making the rest of her profits from the food and drink she provided for her well-to-do clientele of businessmen, politicians and journalists. Victoria's moral reformers hounded Carroll through the courts, but she managed to operate successfully for thirteen years before she returned to the United States in 1913.

Back in Vancouver, it was the goings-on in Alexander Street and the other red light districts that fired the imaginations of the moral crusaders, but prostitution had many venues and most of them were scruffier than the stereotypical brothel. A historian of New York City, Timothy Gilfoyle, catalogues a wide variety of facilities typical of large cities at that time. There were rooms above taverns, cigar stores and barber shops. There were rooms in boarding houses and so-called "houses of assignation" where landlords provided space for short-term rental. There were "panel houses", where confederates hid behind false walls and robbed clients while they were otherwise occupied. There were concert saloons, massage parlours, dance halls and, when nowhere else was available, dark laneways.[42] Vancouver did not exhibit quite this range, but certainly the brothels of Chinatown and Alexander Street were just a taste of what was available. John McLaren's analysis of arrest records provides a profile of the sex trade as it was practised in the city on the eve of the First World War.[43] "Institutional brothels" accommodated anywhere from four to a dozen women, but the majority of prostitutes worked alone or in groups of two or three, meeting their customers in hotels, rooming houses or apartments. The women themselves were usually in their twenties and did not necessarily engage in prostitution full time. Many had jobs as housemaids, waitresses, dressmakers or in other low-paying positions, and supplemented their incomes with sex work. Close to forty-five percent of the women arrested were US born, while thirty-one percent were born in Canada and twenty-three percent in Europe. More than a quarter were of African heritage. Men were arrested in much smaller numbers; from 1912 to 1917, only forty-three men were charged with keeping a bawdy house, procuring or living on the avails, as compared to 377 women.

✳ ✳ ✳

Whether it had any basis in reality—and McLaren suggests that it did not—the white slavery panic in Canada abated with the changes to the Criminal Code in 1913. In Vancouver, where white slavery had been little more than background to the purity debate, public concern about prostitution also seemed to have been allayed. The raids on the Alexander Street houses during 1912–13 were intended as much to placate the abolitionists as to eradicate the trade, and to this end they were successful. Police stepped up their arrests of women for prostitution-related offences and declared that, by 1914, Alexander Street was "closed".[44] Sex workers dispersed to other parts of the city, and the full-throated cry from press and pulpit against prostitution died away. Perhaps the public was distracted by the severe business recession that descended on the city. In 1913, the sustained boom that had fuelled the growth of Vancouver suddenly went bust. As the diplomatic situation in Europe deteriorated, British investors who had been behind much of the expansion withdrew their capital. Hammers fell silent on construction sites; the value of real estate plummetted; businesses failed. Half the lumber mills in the city closed, and unemployment was running at twice the national rate. The outbreak of war in August 1914 did nothing to improve the situation, except to drain off some of the unemployed who hurried to enlist. In this context of war and financial crisis, the "moral panic" that had characterized the discussion of prostitution lost its immediacy. There were things to worry about other than the "social vice". Vancouver's prostitutes, who operated on the margins of the city's downtown, returned to the margins of public consciousness.

Two

THE SOCIAL EVIL BETWEEN THE WARS

In 1919, just a few months after the end of the world war and the horrible influenza epidemic that followed, a twenty-one-year-old Italian immigrant named Joe Celona arrived in Vancouver. Celona settled into the city's Italian community clustered around Union and Prior streets east of Main. Soon he was running a market at the corner of Main and Keefer in partnership with his friend Tony Lombardi, but storekeeping was apparently the least of Celona's enterprises. In 1922 he was convicted of keeping a brothel on Union; the next year he was acquitted of assaulting a police officer. Celona was also reputed to keep one house that provided white women exclusively for Chinese customers. By 1926 he owned a pair of "disorderly houses" near Main, and when one of them was targeted by police he turned it into a bootleg joint and moved his prostitutes to two rooming houses on East Hastings. Celona's criminal record was lengthening and he was well on his way to becoming the notorious "mayor of East Hastings" (as journalists would later call him).

In 1928, a member of the city police commission, T.W. Fletcher, made a series of sensational charges against the city's police force, claiming that officers were taking bribes from underworld figures.

City council appointed a local lawyer, R.S. Lennie, to investigate the allegations. During his inquiry, Lennie listened to 180 hours of testimony from ninety-eight witnesses, much of it documenting the activities of Joe Celona. By this time, Celona was the undisputed king of Vancouver's underworld and the Lennie inquiry was, in part, a response to fears that he enjoyed immunity from the law and was even subverting the elected government through his close relationship with the mayor, Louis Taylor, and the police chief, H.W. Long. Witness after witness was asked about the activities of Celona (whose name was sometimes misspelled as Cellini or Saloni). "Every officer in the city knows him," declared Detective John Robertson. Robertson reported a conversation that he had with Chief Long in which the chief told him that Celona had complained to Mayor Taylor about police harassment of one of his brothels. Long asked Robertson to keep his uniformed men away from Celona's place, suggesting that the order originated with the mayor's office. On another occasion, Celona had bragged to an officer that he was "good friends" with Mayor Taylor and did not have to put up with police "riding his joint". Another witness, Frank Casisa, who ran brothels of his own, claimed to have met Celona in Taylor's company and even to have seen the mayor drunk at one of Celona's parties.[1] Naturally, the newspapers splashed these supposed revelations across their front pages.

For his part, Mayor Taylor told the inquiry that he knew Celona only as the shopkeeper who sold him his cigars, an unbelievable claim given weeks of contrary testimony. Nonetheless, when Commissioner Lennie issued his final report, he exonerated the mayor from any taint of wrongdoing. Taylor had never accepted a bribe, Lennie decided, nor had he interfered with the police on behalf of Joe Celona or any other felon. Lennie, who did not find Casisa to be a reliable informant, saw no reason to accuse the mayor of any crime, or even to suggest that he resign. Still, the report came down hard on Taylor's judgment and administrative competence. It argued that the mayor's "open door policy" of going soft on vice crimes while encouraging police to go after violent criminals was responsible for confusion and low morale in the force. It also confirmed suspicions that Celona operated his brothels and bootleg joints with impunity.[2] Still, the report did not go along with the more alarmist charges that Vancouver was a city of unrestrained vice and immorality. Lennie sympathized with a police force that was understaffed and underpaid compared to those of other cities of comparable size and concluded that, while there were problems, overall the force was doing a creditable job. He could not help citing the testimony of a veteran RCMP officer, A.E. Reames, who when asked to comment on "the moral conditions" of Vancouver said, "I find that Vancouver as a seaport town is one of the cleanest seaports that I have ever been in, so far as crime, serious crime, is concerned." As for prostitution and gambling specifically, Reames said, they "are not any worse than any other city I have been in."[3]

Nonetheless, the Lennie inquiry brought about the downfall of Taylor and Chief Long. In October 1928, less than two months after the inquiry made its report, Taylor entered a civic election campaign against the grocery tycoon William Malkin, who chose to run on the issue of police corruption. According to Malkin, the city was in the grip of "a vicious professional vice ring". The election, he said, was a fight for clean government and safe streets.[4] The voters agreed. They swept a disgraced Taylor, who had already served six terms, out of office and installed a new regime with a mandate to clean house. Chief Long was busted down to traffic division and all the members of his morality squad were suspended.

For Joe Celona, however, business went on as usual. If anything, the Lennie investigation burnished his reputation. Now everyone had heard of the King of the Bawdy Houses. By 1934 Louis Taylor was back in the mayor's office and Celona had solidified his friendship with the new police chief, John Cameron. The mobster and the cop were seen sharing chicken and champagne while touring Howe Sound in the city's police boat, and Celona was known to be a regular visitor to the chief's home and office where the pair allegedly engaged in drinking parties, with booze supplied by a local bootlegger.[5] At the same time, rumours again circulated that Mayor Taylor was mixing with the city's criminal class. Well-known theatre manager Ivan Ackery recalled the red necktie that was Taylor's trademark: "I always wondered whether it was his mischievous way of flaunting his sympathy for the city's prostitutes." Ackery also related a story about Taylor in his memoirs. "A musician of the early thirties remembers that Taylor used to take over the Belmont Cabaret every Sunday evening to entertain his friends. Six nights a week the public danced to Les Crane and his orchestra, but the seventh night belonged to His Honor. Joe Salona [sic], who dealt in the city's illicit trades in those days, would provide the liquor and the ladies."[6]

To the extent that it existed, the cozy relationship between Celona and civic officials came to an abrupt end in 1935. Early that year yet another law-and-order administration took office at city hall. The new mayor was Gerry McGeer, already a prominent political figure. During the 1920s he had represented British Columbia in contentious freight-rate negotiations, and in 1928 he was one of the lawyers who regularly attended the Lennie inquiry hearings, making no secret of his belief that "organized lawlessness has taken charge of this town." McGeer made vice one of the cornerstones of his campaign. According to him, Vancouver was in the hands of the crime bosses, notably Joe Celona, who ran their gambling joints and brothels while the police looked the other way. "I intend to expel the gamblers, racketeers and vice-mongers who are making our city a rendezvous for the criminal class," he promised.[7] One of his election slogans was "I'm Going to Barcelona" [to bar Celona].[8] He easily defeated an aging Louis Taylor, whose claim that he had not been elected to run "a Sunday school city" did not sit well with an electorate roused by alarmist rhetoric. Recognizing that the new mayor meant business, Chief Cameron resigned. According to McGeer, the chief visited his house one night drunk, begging to keep his job, but McGeer wouldn't listen to him. Cameron was charged with corruption, though not convicted. Meanwhile, McGeer, who claimed to have been threatened by the city's mobsters, was followed everywhere by an armed police bodyguard.[9]

The following year Celona, who was still limping from a gunshot wound in the hip inflicted by his wife Josie when she caught him in bed with another woman, was charged with keeping a dozen young women at the Maple Hotel on East Hastings where, according to witnesses, they were visited mainly by Asian men. In April 1935, Celona, just thirty-eight years old, was convicted of procuring, living off the avails, and keeping a disorderly house, and sentenced to twenty-two years in jail, reduced to twelve on appeal.[10] "He may be a clever Italian," prosecutor Dugald Donaghy told the court in his summation. "He may have made a lot of money. But he slipped his foot when he took up his abode on the fourth floor of the Maple Hotel."[11] When authorities released Celona after he had served less than half of his sentence, public protest was so intense that he was returned to the penitentiary to serve the remainder. In 1947 he emerged from prison, and for the rest of his life he dabbled in boot-legging and gambling. He was no longer "the sinister figure in the white slave rackets" that he had been during the inter-war period, but the journalist Jack Wasserman later noted that Celona was "a rough customer who commanded fear among east enders right up until his death" (on 4 March 1958).[12] He was notoriously camera shy. Appearing before another inquiry into police corruption in 1955, he punched a newspaper photographer who was attempting to take his picture.[13] Those who knew Celona agreed that he was a man you did not want to cross. A musician, Austin Phillips, an habitué of East End nightspots during the 1930s, recalled Celona well. "That's a guy you couldn't even be decent with," he said. "And he was just a young man but let go long enough he'd of become another Al Capone."[14]

✳ ✳ ✳

Joe Celona was a big fish in Vancouver's criminal underworld between the wars, and the sea in which he swam was the city's East End. Roughly speaking, this was the neighbourhood along East Hastings and east of Main Street between Prior and the harbour, later known as Strathcona and the Downtown Eastside. The East End was an ethnically mixed working-class neighbourhood, home to immigrant families from Italy, Portugal, Russia and Scandinavia, blacks from the United States and Chinese and Japanese from across the Pacific. A dozen languages might be heard on a stroll through the Main Street farmers' market on a Saturday morning, and the local Strathcona School was commonly known as the League of Nations.[15] The neighbourhood began as a cluster of bungalows and rooming houses close by the Hastings Mill, then expanded steadily south and east as more labouring people were attracted to the workshops, mills and manufactories that located there. One of the largest employers was the nearby BC Sugar refinery established by Benjamin Rogers in 1891. Until 1929, Vancouver was much smaller in area than it is today. Point Grey and South Vancouver were separate municipalities, leaving the city proper to occupy the downtown core between the harbour and False Creek and an area east to Boundary Road and south as far as Sixteenth Avenue. The neighbourhood around Hastings and Main was its hub. "This neighbourhood was the liveliest part of Vancouver in the twenties and thirties," recalled one long-time resident, John Bileck. "From Woodward's to Gore Street [on Hastings] there was activity from early in the morning to the dead of night... There were shops, bootleggers, cafes, panhandlers, bums, everything. Wide open, the city was."[16] City Hall occupied the old market building beside the Carnegie Library on Main Street. The street railway system radiated out from the BC Electric Company's main station at Hastings and Carrall, and thousands of suburbanites were drawn into the area every day to shop at Woodward's department store and take a meal at one of the restaurants on Hastings Street, which was illuminated at night by neon signs (an innovation of the twenties) that buzzed and glowed outside theatres such as the Beacon, the Royal, the Rex, the Princess and the Crystal. The business centre of Vancouver would not shift westward to the Granville Street corridor until the 1950s.

People in other parts of the city—the leafy West End, Shaughnessy with its towered mansions, the well-to-do suburbs of Dunbar and

West Point Grey, the respectable middle- and working-class precincts of Grandview and Kitsilano—associated the East End and its "foreign" population with crime and vice. Its criminal reputation was epitomized in the public mind by a sensational triple killing in March 1917. A black drug addict named Robert Tait barricaded himself in his apartment above a grocery store on East Georgia Street along with his girlfriend, a white prostitute named Frankie Russell. The incident, which began as a dispute over unpaid rent, quickly escalated into a shoot-out when police tried to enter the apartment. After wounding three officers, Tait fired his shotgun out of the front window, killing a nine-year-old boy who happened to be crossing the street to buy candy. Chief Malcolm MacLennan rushed to the scene, along with every other available cop, and after negotiations failed they decided to rush the apartment. The assault team chopped down the door with an axe only to be met with a barrage of gunfire from Tait, who by this time had retreated to a bedroom. MacLennan was fatally wounded and lay bleeding on the kitchen floor while his men retreated back outside. As police and firefighters planned another assault, shots were heard inside the apartment, and a short time later Frankie Russell emerged with her hands up. Tait had shot himself in the head with his shotgun. The murder of a child; the death of a police chief; drugs, race and prostitution—no wonder this incident confirmed every prejudice about life in the East End.

By the 1920s, the area on both sides of Main was known disparagingly as "the square mile of crime" where one went in search of bootleg liquor, gambling and women. Angelo Branca began practising law in an office at Hastings and Main in the mid-1920s and during the 1930s he defended many prostitutes and madams. He recalled that the brothels were well distributed throughout the neighbourhood. "There were one or two along Union Street in the 200 and 300 block, there were some along Gore Avenue between Prior Street and Keefer, there were some along Dunlevy, and there were one or two pretentious joints along Railway Avenue and Alexander Street."[17] By "pretentious joints", Branca meant some holdovers from the heyday of Alexander Street in the era before the Great War. "There was one place that's still on Alexander Street: there was a stairway upstairs there, and a beautiful drawing room with full mirrors that covered the whole bloody wall, all bevelled up, and beautiful furniture and so on." Obviously the brothels of Alexander Street lived on in local legend, polished by memory to a high gloss of sophistication. Another informant, interviewed by Daphne Marlatt and Carole Itter for their invaluable book *Opening Doors: Vancouver's East End*, was David de Camillis, who recalled being a fourteen-year-old delivery boy on Alexander Street during the 1930s.

> The couple [of houses] that I managed to see inside when we did early morning deliveries were absolutely deluxe. Posh. The best. Beautiful wallpaper and a lot of the beds had big curtains behind them, right on the wall, to give the warmth feeling. And beautiful big soft chesterfields. Now these would be the high-class places and you'd go in there with a feeling of extreme wealth. Beautiful glassware, like, for liquor. According to this driver I was with, he said that [the women would] be checked over by a doctor every week, and they were run by a madam. No pimps at all. [...] One madam was a *fantastic* person. She had her own daughters prostituting too. Wonderful clothes. There was no smuttiness in their talking, they

were real ladies. And they had the highest class of clientele [...] they weren't regarded as a base person in the community, because the prostitute of those days had certain morals.[18]

Peter Battistoni, who began delivering bread around the East End for his father's bakery in the 1920s, calculated that there were "130 sporting houses" on his route, seventy around Union Street alone.[19] Max Jaffe, who was a youngster living in Strathcona during the 1930s, recalled how prostitution was part of the daily life of the community. "Along Union there was quite a few houses with girls where men would go. It wasn't a rowdy situation. In fact, I used to walk by on the way to the streetcar and a lot of times wave to them, you know. But it wasn't a centre of evil. If you walked along the street and knew house 'A' was a bootlegging establishment, and house 'B' was a house with girls in it, so what? So people came and went, but it didn't seem to have any influence or direct bearing on your everyday activities or life."[20]

One of the East End madams, Kiyoko Tanaka-Goto, described her operations in an interview. She came to British Columbia during the First World War when she was a nineteen-year-old "picture bride". After four years as a farm labourer and laundress, she moved into Vancouver and went into partnership with three other women. Her first operation was a combined restaurant, "blind pig" and brothel, catering mainly to transient fishermen and loggers. The place was located on a stretch of Powell Street east of Main known to outsiders as "Little Tokyo": a neighbourhood of stores, apartments, barbershops, bathhouses, restaurants, pool halls and gambling clubs owned and patronized by Japanese-Canadians. On nearby Alexander Street, the Japanese Businessmen's Club occupied one of the buildings that once had been a brothel.[21] After a couple of years, Tanaka-Goto moved to Kamloops. When she returned to Vancouver in 1927, she leased the upstairs floor of a hotel on West Hastings and turned the rooms into a brothel. "I hired 12 prostitutes and took commissions. Usually the owner would take 50 percent but I just took 30 percent, so I got on well with the girls, they liked me. Those days you could get a white woman for $2 and a Japanese woman for anywhere from $3 to $5. The Japanese women cost more because they were more in demand." She explained how she handled the police: "If a policeman wanted a woman I arranged it for him. And of course they didn't pay, I paid the girls, but it's cheaper than getting arrested." She ran this operation at 35 West Hastings until she was interned along with all the other Japanese-Canadians during the Second World War.[22] Hers was only one of several brothels on Hastings Street, which was also home to Joe Celona's operation at the Maple Hotel.

At the other end of the neighbourhood was Hogan's Alley, a place you could buy anything: drugs, booze, a weapon, a woman. Gone now, destroyed by the construction of the Georgia Viaduct, it was a scruffy laneway of wooden shacks running east of Main Street between Prior and Union streets. (The name may refer to an actual person, Harry Hogan, an Irishman who was said to have lived there. More probably it is a reference to a nineteenth-century New York newspaper comic strip, "The Yellow Kid", which featured a rough-and-tumble alley of that name. Crime-ridden, urban neighbourhoods in North American cities often received the nickname, and the FBI calls one of its urban tactical training facilities Hogan's Alley.) Wayde Compton, in his book about black British Columbians, calls Hogan's Alley "a black neighbourhood".[23] Certainly this section of town attracted blacks, many of whom worked as porters on the trains that came and went from the nearby stations, but other testimony suggests the alley was racially non-exclusive. "There was every kind of people there," recalled the bread man Peter Battistoni, "Hindus and Negroes and white people." Much as he wanted to blame outsiders for most of the problems, Battistoni had to admit that the alley was a violent spot. "I was delivering there every Monday and almost every Monday you'd find a body. I seen two women dead one day under a barn. One in a garbage can with her feet sticking out. And you'd always find somebody."[24] The musician Austin Phillips recalled that an Italian bootlegger named Lungo was "The King" of the place in the mid-1930s. "There was nothing but parties in Hogan's Alley," he said, "night time, anytime, and Sundays all day. You could go by at six or seven o'clock in the morning, and you could hear jukeboxes going, you hear somebody hammering the piano, playing the guitar, or hear some fighting, or *see* some fighting, screams, and everybody carrying on."[25] Hogan's Alley was a favourite resort of the city's criminal underclass and of thrill-seekers from other neighbourhoods. It was also a place where police officers went in their off hours to gamble, drink and collect the bribes they charged for looking the other way.

Testimony at the Lennie inquiry made it clear that authorities had two objectives when it came to controlling prostitution in the city. The first was to eradicate street prostitution as much as possible. "I wanted to get—and have got pretty well—the street walkers off the street, that is what our chief complaints come from—street walking,"

Chief Long told the commissioner.[26] Officer Charles MacDonald of the morality squad explained that police were more concerned about streetwalkers working out of rooming houses, apartments and hotels than they were about brothels.[27] The second objective was to confine places of prostitution to the East End. Sergeant Roderick Munro reported on a conversation that he had with Chief Long near the end of 1926 during which the chief explicitly told him to try to confine prostitution "to areas downtown"; i.e., the East End.[28] Chief Long himself explained that "there are a number of houses in the east end of the city where the girls live, and whenever I get a complaint about these places they are attended to and watched until there is an act which they can be arrested for. That is the procedure. These girls have to live somewhere, of course."[29] Apparently such complaints were rare, because several witnesses made it clear that the police hardly ever raided these "hookshops". As long as it was carried on discreetly and did not spread into residential neighbourhoods or the Granville Street business district, prostitution was tolerated. Toleration came at a price, of course; witnesses made clear that police routinely accepted payments of $50 a month or more to leave a brothel alone. The same was true for gambling joints. When, for appearance's sake, police raided a gambling den or a hookshop, operators were usually tipped off in advance. As far as Lennie could determine, the money collected in this way did not go into the pockets of individual officers but was handed into a fund used to pay for the force's social events.

At times, testimony from the Lennie hearings reads like something out of a Ring Lardner story, as witnesses describe the activities of brothel keepers named "French Pete", "Tom the Greek", "The Mole", and Shue Moy, the most prominent Chinatown gambling kingpin. The women themselves remain largely anonymous. A veteran vice cop named Joe Ricci calculated that about seventy-five percent of the prostitutes in the city worked for pimps, whose control over them was near absolute. The career of one young prostitute reveals the dark side of the business. She told Commissioner Lennie that she worked in a brothel above a barbershop on Main Street where the owner routinely beat her when business was slow. One beating caused her to give birth prematurely. Later, after becoming pregnant again, she ended up in hospital after a botched abortion. On her release, she returned to the brothel where the owner beat her black and blue. At the same time, during the 1920s, the owner was paying protection money to the police every month.[30]

The Great Depression descended on Vancouver with a suddenness that left bewildered government officials not knowing how to respond. The stock market crash of October 1929 was followed by a drop in commodity prices, disastrous for an economy such as British Columbia's that relied on the export of raw resources. The demand for BC fish, forest products, fruit and minerals fell sharply. Unemployed men, most of them single, began drifting into the city from the Interior. For job seekers from other parts of the country as well, Vancouver was the end of the line. Destitute transients gathered in squatters' camps, the so-called hobo jungles, on the harbourfront and beside the train tracks. Vancouver "is the Mecca of the unemployed", one official reported. "They are attracted here by milder weather conditions and the prospects of obtaining some kind of work throughout the Winter."[31] But work was not available. Instead, the jobless stood in breadlines, went door to door looking for hand-outs, stalked the downtown sidewalks begging for spare change. Vancouver always had attracted the unemployed during the winter months because of the seasonal nature of the provincial economy, but the number arriving in the early months of 1930 was unprecedented. Advocates for the jobless, some of them communists, organized parades and demonstrations, beginning with the occupation of the Cambie Street government relief office in mid-December 1929. In January, an unprecedented flurry of protests convulsed the city, culminating in a mass demonstration by about 300 people at the Powell Street Grounds (now Oppenheimer Park) at the end of the month. Police attacked the demonstrators with whips and truncheons and arrested seven militants, four of whom were later convicted of unlawful assembly. The determination of the unemployed, and their anger at the apparent indifference of authorities, continued to grow.

Attempts to deal with the unemployment crisis met with little success. Relief programmes, whether they offered labouring jobs at starvation wages or direct cash payments, placed a heavy burden on the city's treasury. The Liberal prime minister, William Lyon Mackenzie King, dealt with the problem by ignoring it. Suggesting that unemployment was a scheme cooked up by his political opponents, he infamously declared that he "would not give a single cent" for relief to provincial Conservative governments, of which British Columbia's was one. Canadians made King pay by voting him out of office in July 1930, but the new Conservative administration of R.B. Bennett had no more success in attempting to turn around the economy. While the three levels of government—civic, provincial and federal—dickered over who would bear the cost of relief, unemployment soared. At the beginning of 1931 the jobless rate in

British Columbia reached twenty-seven percent, the highest in the country.

As the large numbers of unemployed who had migrated to Vancouver grew increasingly restive, the authorities grew increasingly repressive. All public meetings and parades without a special permit were banned. The Powell Street Grounds were designated as the only place that outdoor public meetings could take place. At the end of January 1931, when demonstrators gathered in Victory Square downtown, police waded into the crowd with clubs swinging and arrested ten men. In September, city council closed the hobo jungles, alarmed at the health risk they posed and certain that they attracted transients from other parts of the country. That autumn the province opened the first of its rural work camps designed to isolate the unemployed away from urban centres and keep them busy at menial jobs for as little as twenty cents a day. Later these camps were absorbed into the federal government camps administered by the Department of National Defence.

Theatre manager Ivan Ackery recalled the depths of the Depression in Vancouver. "Beggars went from house to house, looking for meals or handouts. The streets were filled with people just wandering around in despair, many past even trying to help themselves."[32] The city itself faced the prospect of bankruptcy. Because a growing number of homeowners defaulted on their tax payments, civic revenues fell sharply. The neighbouring municipalities of Burnaby and North Vancouver (city and district) handed management of their affairs over to a provincial commissioner. Would Vancouver be forced to do the same? Like everyone else, Vancouver's prostitutes must have felt the impact of hard economic times as the number of men who could afford their services dropped while more women were being drawn into the business by joblessness and destitution. According to a police estimate there were one hundred brothels operating in 1933, accommodating about the same number of prostitutes as police had reported in the late twenties.[33] Meanwhile, the situation in the rural work camps deteriorated. Men did not enjoy living under military discipline in spartan conditions with no prospect of improvement. Towards the end of 1934 they began leaving the camps for Vancouver, alarming authorities with their street protests and demonstrations once again.

Against this backdrop of economic crisis and civic strife, Gerry McGeer won election as Vancouver's mayor in December 1934. To carry out his proclaimed war on crime he appointed a new police chief, Colonel W.W. Foster, who had been an engineer, a former Conservative member of the legislature, a war hero and a mountaineer but never a policeman. However surprising, the choice was nonetheless inspired. Foster ended up serving longer than any chief since before the Great War (leaving in 1940 to rejoin the army) and established himself as an energetic crime-buster who shared the mayor's distaste for gangsters and so-called communists. The conviction of the notorious Joe Celona was considered a triumph for the force, as was the chief's firm handling of unemployed protesters. When thousands of the latter gathered in Victory Square on 23 April 1935, Foster, fearing a communist-led insurgency, advised Mayor McGeer to read the Riot Act and disperse the crowd. Foster's men later broke up meetings and arrested activists in a determined effort to break the back of what the red-baiting McGeer called "one of the most persistent and flagrant attempts at revolutionary disorder ever undertaken in a Canadian city."[34] As an act of political repression, the episode was equalled three years later on "Bloody

Sunday", 19 June 1938, when Foster's men, aided by the RCMP, used tear-gas, whips and clubs to end a month-long occupation of the city post office by militant unemployed.

Not long after taking the chief's job, Foster solidified his reputation as a fearless defender of law and order when he took part in a sensational running gunfight through the city. During the summer of 1935, a gang of robbers was victimizing small groceries and drug stores. The newspapers dubbed them the "Silk Stocking Gang" for their stocking masks, or the "Blue Sedan Bandits" because they preferred to carry out their holdups in stolen blue sedans. Foster was known to tour the city at night in the back of a squad car with his driver, a constable named McKinnon. One September night the chief's car was crossing the Granville Street bridge when news came over the radio that the gang had just knocked over another store. A few moments later the getaway car hurtled past in the opposite direction. The two cops made a U-turn and began a pursuit, exchanging gunfire with the robbers as they sped down Broadway. The chase continued for several minutes until the driver of the getaway car lost control and crashed. Four men emerged from the wrecked vehicle. McKinnon shot and captured one. The other three fled on foot, but two of them were later taken into custody. Together the men were convicted of twenty-eight robberies, giving the police a huge publicity boost. Foster's bullet-riddled car was testament to his determination to clean up the city.[35]

According to Mayor McGeer, Vancouver was in thrall to the criminal classes. Chief Foster did not disagree. After just two weeks in office he reported that "the condition in Vancouver is a disgraceful one as regards crime and vice", largely because of the previous regime's "open town" policy. Regarding prostitution, Foster described "certain houses of the vilest character, which Police Officers dared not enter, and to which are taken and kept for the use of the Chinese, young girls usually around the age of 15, the majority of whom have been enticed or abducted from their homes by vicious characters well known to be the ring leaders in Vancouver of this horrible traffic." Deploying the rhetoric of white slavery, he concluded that "Vancouver has become the International Headquarters of a revolting type of vice, and the natural refuge for criminals of dangerous character."[36] A month later, the police chief's legal advisor, T.G. McLelan, reported in a similar vein, raising the spectre of young girls forcibly enslaved in brothels where they were "ravaged by Orientals." "The despicable crime of white slavery has become so rampant in the City under the lack of police intervention, that the ring-leaders have brazenly defied the law," McLelan told the mayor. The conviction of Joe Celona that spring was considered an important blow against the "merchants of vice", as were a series of police raids on brothels carried out on Foster's initiative. By autumn, the pumped-up election-time rhetoric had given way to a more sanguine view of prostitution in the city. A memo signed by Foster, the city prosecutor and a police magistrate declared that the activities of pimps and brothel keepers "have practically ceased".

It is suggested that the Police Force make every reasonable effort toward the suppression of anything in the business [prostitution] which is of the nature of a public nuisance, particularly street-walking, and those houses where window-tapping takes place, and brothels which may be said to be a nuisance in their community [...] and also any which are found in residential areas. It is realized of course that this evil cannot be entirely stamped out, and that the efforts of the Police should be directed to stamping out its most objectionable features...[37]

In other words, the memo recommended the same policy of toleration and control that police were following since long before McGeer chose to make it an election issue. Nevertheless, McGeer was able to claim victory in his war on vice. He declared 3 January 1936, a Sunday, to be a day of prayer and humiliation and called on the public to go to their churches to thank God "for the removal of commercialized vice and the return of peace and order."[38]

✳ ✳ ✳

During the interwar period, Chinatown continued to haunt the imagination of white Vancouver. It was, to outsiders, a depraved place where vices of all kinds flourished: gambling, drugs, prostitution. "It has been proved [...] that the traffic in habit-forming drugs centres in Chinatown," claimed the *Sun* in 1920, and the *Daily World* painted a lurid picture for its readers of white women being taxied to "Chinese labour camps and lodging houses" to prostitute themselves to earn money for drugs.[39] Chinatown was compared to a contagion that threatened to spread its immorality to the rest of the city. Newspaper editors worried that industrious Asian farmers and businessmen would soon control the provincial economy. An attorney general of the province, Alex Manson, campaigned vigorously for an all-white hiring policy by the province's employers.[40] Asian Canadians were not allowed to vote, and in 1923 the federal government replaced its infamous "head tax" with the Chinese Immigration Act, excluding almost all Chinese from immigrating to

Canada. (There was already a gentlemen's agreement in place with the government of Japan limiting the flow of Japanese immigration.) People of Asian heritage could not work in the provincial civil service and were banned from most professions. They were also discouraged from moving into most of Vancouver's residential suburbs. There was no embarrassment in proclaiming one's support for a "White British Columbia".

Three books published by prominent writers during the 1920s capture the virulent antagonism that the white majority felt towards Asian Canadians, particularly the Chinese. Hilda Glynn-Ward was the nom de plume of Mrs. Hilda Williams Howard, a Welsh-born freelance writer based in Victoria. In 1921 the *Sun* published her novel *The Writing on the Wall*, in which she prophesied a great "race war" between Chinese and Japanese for control of British Columbia once whites had been demoralized by drugs and miscegenation and killed off by typhoid intentionally spread by Chinese greengrocers.[41] The following year, Emily Murphy, an Alberta magistrate and popular writer under the pseudonym Janey Canuck, published *The Black Candle*, a supposed exposé of the drug trade in Canada. In it, she painted a lurid picture of Vancouver's Chinatown which, she claimed, was headquarters for "the most powerful and wealthy criminal organization on the American continent". According to Murphy, the Chinese were using drugs to bring about "the downfall of the white race" and take control of the world.[42] The third and possibly most influential anti-Asian propagandist was a Vancouver lawyer and poet named Thomas MacInnes. The scion of a prominent BC political family—his father was a senator and served a term as lieutenant governor—he wrote a series of anti-Asian articles in the local press that formed the basis of his 1927 book

Oriental Occupation of British Columbia. His pet cause was the restriction of Asian-owned businesses. In Vancouver, he argued, Asians were expanding out of the Chinese and Japanese neighbourhoods and threatening to take over the entire commercial downtown. "Time will not cure the evil of Oriental penetration of British Columbia, with its menace of economic conquest," he wrote, "unless drastic action be taken without delay to offset it."[43] Even though people of Japanese and Chinese descent made up only seven percent of the population of the province, all three of these influential commentators warned that white British Columbia was under dire threat from them.

Of particular concern to outsiders was the fate of white womanhood when exposed to the contaminating influence of the "Oriental", chiefly in Vancouver's Chinatown. In order to protect white women from corruption, a city bylaw made it illegal for Chinese-owned businesses to employ white females, and in 1923 the province passed the Women and Girls Protection Act, which criminalized the employment of white women by anyone "if local police officials deemed it inadvisable". This legislation avoided singling out the Chinese, but they were its main target.[44] Even as the population of Chinatown declined by half as a result of the new immigration restrictions, white Vancouver continued to fret about the moral peril the Chinese posed to its women. The issue came to a head in 1937 in one of the most unusual workers' protests of the Depression.

For years, Chinese restaurant and tea-house owners had been importing young women from China to work as waitresses. In a predominantly male community, these cafés attracted customers easily. The waitresses served tea and food, chatted with the patrons, and sometimes made further arrangements. "The waitresses made good money in those days, twenty to twenty-five dollars a week plus tips," explained Lun Yee, who worked in such restaurants during this period. "The waitresses didn't have to go with everyone, they would pick and choose only the good-looking men to go with. Of course, they had to give part of their earnings to their owners."[45] By no means did all of the waitresses go out with customers, or prostitute themselves if they did. Denise Chong, in her family memoir of Chinatown, describes the example of her grandmother, who struggled to raise three children on her own. "Her motive in these casual liaisons was mainly to help ease her financial problems, yet it was not prostitution in the strict sense of a simple, quick exchange of sexual acts for money. The men would generously pay a gambling debt here or there or give her money to 'buy herself something.'"[46]

By the 1930s, with the ban on Chinese immigration having an effect on the availability of Chinese women, Chinatown restaurateurs were hiring white women to work as waitresses, even though doing so was technically illegal. So long as no one objected, the police looked the other way. But in 1935 Mayor McGeer and Chief Foster took up the cause of moral purity in Chinatown as part of their more generalized campaign against vice. Many whites considered the job of Chinatown waitress to be a euphemism for prostitute, or at least the first step on the slippery path to immorality. Using the powers of the Women and Girls Protection Act, the police ordered several restaurants to let go their white waitresses. According to Foster, the action was necessary because Chinese owners were forcing their white employees into prostitution. When the provincial legislation turned out to be an unreliable legal weapon, the police began using municipal licensing regulations to achieve the same purpose. Owners of Chinatown restaurants were told to either fire their white waitresses or face the cancellation of their business licences.

Chinatown business leaders fought back with petitions and appeals, and so did the waitresses themselves. On 24 September 1937, more than two dozen women employed by the restaurants paraded to Vancouver's city hall to protest the policies that were costing them their jobs. The problem, they claimed, was "a bunch of fussy old bridge-playing gossips who are self-appointed directors of morals for the girls in Chinatown... We must live and heaven knows if a girl is inclined to go wrong, she can do it just as readily on Granville Street as she can down here."[47] But this piece of common sense bore no weight with Mayor George Miller (McGeer's first term had expired at the end of 1936 and he had not run for a second) who refused to see the protestors or to meliorate the policy. The ban on white waitresses in Chinatown held.[48]

✳ ✳ ✳

If prostitutes threatened the moral foundations of the community, they also threatened its health. Public concern about the spread of venereal disease dates back to the First World War when it was discovered that a surprising number of Canadian soldiers were infected with gonorrhea and syphilis, not all of it picked up overseas. In 1915, the infection rate climbed as high as twenty-eight percent among the men in the Canadian Expeditionary Force. Naturally the military was alarmed but so were civilian health officials, who worried that returning soldiers would infect Canadian women. Governments were mobilized and in March 1918 Ontario passed legislation to combat what the Toronto *Globe* called "the secret plague".[49] The new law required anyone infected with a venereal disease to seek treatment or face a fine. It also allowed medical officers to compel treatment, and provided for fines for anyone who knowingly infected another person. Along with all the other provinces, British Columbia passed similar legislation in April 1919.[50] Following the war, health officials continued to wage a campaign against VD, establishing the Canadian National Council for Combatting Venereal Disease (later the Canadian Social Hygiene Council) to educate the public about the perils of sex. Prostitutes were singled out as a main source of disease. Women appearing in court on prostitution-related charges were examined at a clinic.[51] "Prostitution cannot be made safe," declared one government pamphlet, and the public was encouraged to believe that all prostitutes were infected.[52] The Social Hygiene Council had offices in Victoria and Vancouver where it organized lectures and distributed educational material.

In British Columbia, the problem of venereal disease and prostitution came to be associated with the beer parlour. Following the province's brief experiment with prohibition between 1917 and 1921, the sale and consumption of liquor was regulated by the government. Alcohol was sold only at government liquor stores, and drinking establishments had to be licensed by the three-member Liquor Control Board. In general, consumption was discouraged; in practice, it thrived, thanks to bootleggers and "beer clubs", bars that masqueraded as social or service clubs. By the mid-1920s, public support for drinking establishments that would sell "beer by the glass" was so strong that the government eased its restrictions, and in March 1925 the first hotel beer parlours opened. By the end of the year, Vancouver had sixty-five of them in the downtown core alone. Drinkers of a certain age will remember these dimly-lit watering holes, reeking of tobacco smoke and stale beer, because they remained British Columbia's main venue for public drinking for decades. There was no standing at the bar, no hard liquor, no food, no entertainment, no singing or darts or billiards, nothing to suggest that consuming alcohol might be enjoyable. Intended to discourage drinking, these proscriptions instead promoted it because, as Robert Campbell points out, "in a beer parlour there was little to do except drink."[53] Authorities never could decide whether to shield the parlours from public view or open them to public inspection, so windows were either heavily curtained or open to the gazes of passersby. For a brief period women were not allowed in beer parlours. Then, in 1927, a separate room was added to accommodate women drinking alone or with escorts.

Middle-class moralists were suspicious of what went on in beer parlours. By the late 1930s, with concern about venereal disease again on the rise, suspicion had hardened into certainty: the beer parlour was a den of vice where drunken customers were preyed on by diseased prostitutes. "The prostitute is the main root and source of venereal disease in this province," declared Dr. D.H. Williams, the director of venereal disease control.[54] Prostitution was "a community fester from which spreads venereal disease, suffering and death."[55] Williams targeted brothels and beer parlours as the main source of contagion and used his position to campaign vigorously for the suppression of both. When the war broke out, he began to characterize "parlour prostitutes" as a "fifth column", an internal enemy sapping the country's strength by infecting potential soldiers. "The business of commercialized prostitution must go!" he blared.

"National Defence demands it!"[56] To further segregate the sexes in the parlours, hotels were required to place a partition between the men and the ladies and escorts.

To a degree, city officials fell in with Williams's zealotry. In January 1939, another newly elected mayor, Dr. Lyle Telford, launched yet another crackdown on vice, ordering the closure of a number of "disorderly houses" and keeping a close eye on activity in the beer parlours. Given Telford's personal history, he seems to have been unsuited to the role of anti-vice crusader. He was a socialist firebrand who had served as a CCF member of the legislature and was well known in the city for his radio talks advocating a variety of progressive policies. In 1932 he had risked going to jail by opening Canada's second birth control clinic, which dispensed condoms and other contraceptive devices. His partner in operating the clinic was Frances Moren, for whom he left his wife in a highly public divorce scandal. For all these reasons, Telford might have been expected to be sympathetic to the fate of prostitutes who were hounded out of business, but he was firm in his desire to eradicate vice from the city.

People who worked for social service agencies realized that the police crackdown on brothels was going to throw a number of young women into the streets. At the invitation of the ecumenical General Ministerial Association, representatives of various welfare groups met to discuss what they might do, with the result that in mid-1939 the Hostel for Prostitutes opened its doors on West Eleventh Avenue. This facility, dedicated to the care and reform of prostitutes, provided rooms for as many as six women at a time. It was supported by the city's social service department, the provincial health and welfare department and the John Howard Society, with donations from other organizations, and was operated by a committee of female social workers. The hostel provided food, shelter and religious and moral counselling. In the event, few if any former prostitutes sought help there. The hostel catered chiefly to young women who were considered promiscuous or incorrigible, and it closed at the end of 1945 because it was not really being used by anyone at all.[57]

The 1939 raids constituted another of the anti-vice campaigns that broke out in the city with clockwork regularity. Whether it was politicians looking for an election issue, moral reformers looking for vice-free streets or public health activists looking for a disease-free community, someone was always looking to drive the prostitutes out of business. Usually they succeeded only in driving them into another venue or another part of the city. Angelo Branca, who as a lawyer had a lot of professional experience with the issue, observed the results of the 1939 crackdown. "The problems started to come with the last World War," he recalled, "when, for fear that the army personnel would be infected with venereal diseases, they started to bang down on [brothels and beer parlours] and the result of that was that we had girls all over the bars and the streets and so on, and no real method of controlling them."[58] The all-too familiar pattern was working itself out in a new context of depression and war. Official policy oscillated between controlled toleration and moral zeal. When the latter was in the ascendancy, prostitutes were rousted from the brothels, hustled off the sidewalks, charged as inmates or vagrants, fined, sometimes jailed, then released into the community to start the process over again. Once an aroused public was satisfied that "something had been done", the status quo would return, which is to say that prostitution was tolerated in certain neighbourhoods so long as the participants did nothing to draw attention to themselves.

Three

FROM BROTHELS TO BARS:
PROSTITUTION IN THE POSTWAR CITY

Nobody ever won election as mayor of Vancouver on a platform promising to improve the lives of prostitutes. On the contrary, several civic politicians had great success promising to do just the opposite. Thomas Neelands, William Malkin, Gerry McGeer and Lyle Telford all discovered that it was good politics to launch a war on vice. So in 1946, when McGeer decided to return to civic politics by taking another run at the mayor's job, he surprised no one when he came out swinging against the shadowy underworld. Ten years earlier McGeer had declared the streets of Vancouver swept clean of vice. Now he was back, claiming that criminals were operating with impunity in the city once again. "Get going, you thugs," he warned, "because I'm coming again, and there's no room in town for you!"[1] Once elected, he lost no time dumping the police chief, Alex McNeill, and installing his own favourite, Walter Mulligan, with instructions to carry out a thorough house-cleaning. The police commission, on the advice of Mulligan, suspended several experienced officers, who appealed their firings. The public hearings that resulted in March 1947 revealed the by-now familiar pattern of bribes and kickbacks from the city's gamblers and brothel keepers. In the end, twenty-six members of the force lost their jobs or were demoted, and Mulligan, at forty-two the youngest chief in the city's history, was firmly in charge. (No one possibly could have been surprised when, eight years later, Mulligan was implicated in his own corruption scandal involving bribes from bootleggers and gamblers; after being relieved of his job he decamped for California, where he found work at a flower nursery outside Los Angeles.[2])

When they weren't embroiled in scandal, Vancouver police went about the business of controlling prostitution much as they had traditionally, confining it to certain neighbourhoods and tolerating it up to a degree. There had always been laws on the books prohibiting, or at least curtailing, the activities of prostitutes. In the postwar era as earlier, pimping, procuring and living off the avails of prostitution were illegal, though difficult to prosecute since the women were reluctant to testify against men who were often their husbands or boyfriends, and customers had little interest in co-operating. Running or frequenting a "common bawdy house" was also illegal, a bawdy house being defined in the law as a place "kept or occupied, or resorted to by one or more persons for the purpose of prostitution or the practice of acts of indecency." The main statute dealing with street prostitution was the vagrancy provision of the federal Criminal Code, which prohibited a woman from being in a public place if she was unable to "give a good account of herself". This was the infamous "Vag. C.", named for Section 175(1)(c) of the Code, meant to give police the ability to keep prostitutes off the streets. "If we saw women who were obviously prostitutes, we wouldn't go and charge them but we would stop them and take their name and write down on a check card our observations and then we warned them," explained one retired police officer, Bill Harkema, who began walking the beat on the Downtown Eastside in the mid-1960s. "And we'd write down 'warned vag. C'. Then the vice squad could use the check cards to prove 'commonality' [that is, a persistent pattern of behaviour]. A lot of the young guys I worked with saw this as a good way of supplementing their income, by getting overtime to go to court. Lots of guys spent a lot of their careers trying to nail prostitutes."[3]

For men seeking to buy sex but fearful of police entrapment, the alternative to patronizing a brothel or picking up a woman on the street was only a phone call away. During the 1950s, many hotels featured prostitutes on their room-service menus. A word in the ear of a bellhop or a cabbie could produce a phone number or, more directly, a visit from a young woman. Early in January 1959 the *Sun* revealed details of one such operation in a front-page exposé. "A lucrative and wide-open call girl system is flourishing in Vancouver," announced the paper.[4] The *Sun* had dispatched a dozen reporters to different hotels and motels round the city where they had had no trouble at all ordering in prostitutes, in one case phoning the dispatcher at a cab company directly.

Prompted in part by these revelations, police began an investigation of the call-girl racket and in November 1960 raided an Alberni Street apartment that was the nerve centre of one of the major operations. Calls were received from customers or intermediaries, and women were dispatched by cab to various hotels as well as to two Bute Street apartments used for assignations. Cabbies received $7.50 for every john they produced. The women charged $25 an hour or $100 for a night, and got to keep half. The city prosecutor, Stewart McMorran, claimed that one woman made sixty-three visits in one month and earned nearly $2,000.[5] Call-girl operations were almost impossible to prosecute using the vagrancy provisions of the Criminal Code since participants did not make contact in public places. Raids such as this one, which resulted in charges of conspiring to live off the avails of prostitution, represented a new response by police to the limitations of Vag. C, but as an extensive investment of time and personnel was necessary to blow one call-girl setup, police were powerless to stamp it out altogether, even had they wanted to.

The increased incidence of call-girl operations, which were prototypes for the escort agencies that developed twenty years later, was an indication that following the Second World War the bawdy house had ceased to be the main locale for commercial sex in Vancouver. Not that the brothel disappeared entirely. Despite the claim by Police Chief George Archer in 1958 that "there are no bawdy houses open in the city", the press periodically carried reports of raids and arrests.[6] Still, it was apparent that prostitution was increasingly decentralized and deinstitutionalized in the fifties and sixties as women began working out of a variety of venues, including beer parlours, hotels, apartment blocks and nightclubs such as the Cave Supper Club on Hornby Street. At the same time, street prostitutes were pretty well confined to the streets of the East End, where police tolerated their presence. These decades represent a ceasefire in the war on prostitution that had been going on and off since the city's creation. It was a ceasefire that would not last, but while it did, prostitution more or less disappeared from the public agenda.

City of Vancouver Archives / xxxx

Dupont Street circa 1906, the year before its name was changed to East Pender. During the day it was "a bustle of Chinese vegetable vendors and drovers leading herds of cattle." But after dark "the red lights winked on and the wood sidewalks filled with mobs of men in search of drink and companionship."

Vancouver Public Library 20366

After moralists shut down the Dupont Street brothels, attention shifted to Shanghai Alley (shown here in a 1940s view) where "antagonism towards prostitution became mixed with the anti-Asian sentiment so strong in the city."

In the period between the world wars (the photo here was taken in 1935), the Maple Hotel at 177 East Hastings was, among other things, a brothel operated by the underworld kingpin Joe Celona, a camera-shy Italian immigrant. "Those who knew Celona agreed that he was a man you did not want to cross."

City of Vancouver Archives 99-2861

Unlike one of his predecessors, Police Chief W.W. Foster was not a drinking buddy of Joe Celona. On the contrary, this hysterical anti-communist fear monger believed that "the condition in Vancouver is a disgraceful one as regards crime and vice." He engineered Celona's downfall, thus altering the face of prostitution in Vancouver—without of course stamping it out.

Joe Philliponi (left) and his brother Ross Filiponni (the family members born in Canada used a different spelling) outside the Penthouse Cabaret on Seymour Street. The Penthouse was a favourite haunt of movie stars and the centre of the local sex trade. Police misguidedly forced its closure in 1975. Philliponi was later murdered.

Vancouver Police Centennial Museum and Archives P03593

With the Penthouse gone, prostitutes were returning to the streets, where they were more easily harassed than protected.

Nick Didlick, courtesy of the Vancouver Sun

A 1978 federal Supreme Court ruling held that solicitation had to be "pressing and persistent" to be illegal. This emboldened streetwalkers, who congregated along certain "tracks" in the West End, as in this 1992 photo of Nelson Street.

Peter Battistoni, courtesy of the *Vancouver Sun*

When prostitution spread into areas such as Mount Pleasant, "the people who lived there were not happy to see their neighbourhood becoming 'the new West End'". Protests erupted.

Beginning in the 1970s, and with increasing speed in the 1980s and 1990s, the higher-end sex trade moved back indoors. The change was made possible partly because sex-workers were free to advertise in alternative newspapers, particularly the weeklies (and later on the Internet). This also encouraged entrepreneurs to establish elaborate massage parlours with such names as Madame Cleo's, the Platinum Club and the Swedish Touch.

Stephen Osborne

Peter Battistoni, courtesy of the *Vancouver Sun*

The history of prostitution in Vancouver is inseparable from the story of municipal politics, with its phoney crusades and colourful individualists. An example of the latter (shown in a 1978 photo) was Jamie Lee Hamilton, who became a transgendered advocate for sex trade workers' rights. In 2005 she claimed to have had a twelve-year relationship with a candidate for mayor. Legal action resulted.

Mark van Manen, courtesy of the *Vancouver Sun*

The mean age of Vancouver sex trade workers appeared to fall as street prostitution became decentralized. Here teenage hookers are photographed surreptitiously in 1986 along the notorious Davie Street track.

Steve Bosch, courtesy of the *Vancouver Sun*

Street prostitutes from the Downtown Eastside began vanishing in the late 1970s, but authorities were slow to link the disappearances to a serial killer, despite demonstrations by sex trade workers and other women, such as this one in 1999, when twenty-three were known to have gone missing.

When the Royal Canadian Mounted Police circulated this poster later in 1999, the total number of women missing from the streets of the Downtown Eastside stood at thirty-one. The total peaked at sixty-eight, but dropped when two of the women turned up alive.

June 6, 2002: the day a joint police task force, assisted by archaeologists and other specialized experts, began digging up a hog farm in Port Coquitlam, seeking evidence. The owner of the property, Robert William (Willy) Pickton, was charged with the deaths of twenty-seven of the missing women.

RCMP

Richard Lam, courtesy of the *Vancouver Sun*

In the years following the Second World War, the East End, or at least the portion of it between Hastings and the harbourfront, secured its identity as the city's skid road (or Skid Row). Originally, the term referred to the corduroy roads along which logs were skidded out of the forest. Later it came to identify a part of town frequented by loggers in from the bush looking for a room, a bar and a woman, not necessarily in that order. When they grew too infirm to work in the camps, some of these men retired to rooming houses and humble cabins in the East End where they subsisted on their meagre savings or, if they were old enough, their government pension. This had been part of the order of things since Vancouver's earliest days. During the period of economic growth that followed the war, however, skid road became identified as an area of urban blight and a source of embarrassment for people in the city who never went there. Typical of this uptown attitude was a series of articles that appeared in the *Province* in November 1952. One headline blared "Skid Road – Street of Lost Souls Vancouver's Shame". The series, written by a reporter named Bill Ryan, described the neighbourhood as the source of ninety percent of the city's crime, home to hopeless alcoholics and impoverished pensioners, a training ground for dropout teens on their way to becoming young offenders and the heart of the drug traffic. Ryan reported that skid road was "the core of what prostitution is left in Vancouver", which he thought was not much, though every other "social disorder" was thriving in the area.[7] Perhaps most importantly from the point of view of civic officials, the articles pointed out that the city spent about twice as much money on services to the area as it received back in tax revenue.

Downtown residents from this period concur that the East End was home to a tough working-class population that found its entertainment on the streets and in the beer parlours. Peter Trower was one of the loggers who descended on postwar Vancouver to blow off steam after a stint in the bush. In his novel *Dead Man's Ticket*, he evokes a neighbourhood of beer parlours and flophouses fuelled by booze and drugs.

> The usual crew of tenderloin regulars thronged the sidewalk around me—knots of carousing loggers lurching noisily from bar to bar; shabbily dressed East End housewives looking for bargains at the Army and Navy or the Save-on-Meat store; scrofulous winos with grimy paws cadging dimes in raspy voices; cut-rate hookers wearily heading for toast and black coffee at some greasy spoon café; a furtive heroin pusher bound for the Broadway Hotel—Vancouver's notorious "Corner"—to set up shop at a dim beer parlour table; a native girl emerging from a fleabag walk-up with a black eye and a bleary, bemused look; morose old men who were neither bums, drunks nor junkies but simply trapped in this ghetto through poverty, poor health or ill fortune, gazing wistfully from dirty-curtained third-storey windows...[8]

In conversation, Trower recollected that there were plenty of bars, illicit booze cans and down-at-the-heels hotels where prostitutes loitered. For the most part, he said, he stayed away from these women, fearing VD, but he recalled one incident when he and a fellow logger took two women back to their hotel room only to wake up to find the women gone, along with the money he had been saving for a new chainsaw. The "Corner" Trower refers to in his novel was the intersection of Hastings and Columbia, which was a drug bazaar of sorts. He thought that most of the street prostitutes working down on skid road were heroin addicts, hustling to satisfy their habit. Women also went up the coast aboard the Union Steamships coast fleet, claiming to be selling magazine subscriptions in the logging camps.[9]

John Turvey was a teenager when he arrived in the East End from his home in the Fraser Valley in 1957. Turvey, who later was awarded the Order of Canada for his years on the street as a social worker, began as a street hustler in the neighbourhood. He recalled that along Main Street south of Hastings "there were a lot of working women, a *lot* of women... The whole area was women." Operating out of hotels and rooming houses, they catered to a clientele largely of fishermen, loggers and other single men, most of whom were at least seasonal residents of the East End. "There were certainly people from out of the area coming in, tricking with the women, but not to the degree that there is now [mid-1980s]."[10]

The image of the East End as a malignant centre of vice and decay that was also a sinkhole for tax dollars was intensified by postwar economic changes in this part of the city. As hinterland industries such as logging and mining became less dependent on seasonal labour, the transient workforce that for so many years had resorted to the East End during the off-season became less of a presence. At the same time, many businesses (fish plants, mills, wood-product firms, warehouses and shipyards) that had concentrated along the waterfront on Burrard Inlet and in False Creek relocated to cheaper land farther from the downtown core. (Noticeable by their absence as well were the 9,000 members of the city's Japanese-Canadian community who had been forcibly relocated away from the coast during the war.) Another significant change was the shift in transportation facilities.

Since the beginning of the century, vessels of the Union Steamships fleet came and went from the company wharf at the foot of Carrall Street. Union steamers provided freight and passenger service to all the remote corners of the coast, returning to offload scores of loggers, cannery workers and summer excursionists into the nearby downtown streets. Not far away, the ferry from North Vancouver disgorged loads of passengers several times a day. Three blocks south, at the corner of Carrall and Hastings, the BC Electric Company had its main terminal where the large interurban trams sped to and from Richmond, New Westminster and the Fraser Valley.

Whether by land or by water, thousands of people arrived every day in the East End to shop, run errands, see friends, go to the theatre. But then, in the late 1950s, the ferry from the North Shore stopped running, Union Steamships sold its fleet and went out of business, and BC Electric left its Carrall Street station (where the interurbans had stopped running anyway) for a new headquarters on Burrard. As a result of all these changes, the East End, and its skid road in particular, lost much of its economic vitality. The city's commercial centre of gravity shifted westward away from Hastings to Granville Street. By 1966 the *Sun* was describing central Hastings Street as a strip of "cheap hotels, dingy beer parlours, shooting galleries, the claptrap that spells decay", and the streets around were generally viewed by outsiders as an impoverished ghetto of vice. "Once the romping grounds of thousands of loggers, skid road today is a haven for the rejects of society," the *Sun* reported.[11]

Civic planners and politicians responded to the deterioration of the East End by proceeding with plans to demolish it, what one historian has called "urban surgery, without the consent of the patient".[12] The neighbourhood was classified as a blighted area, a slum, which had to be reclaimed through redevelopment. The redevelopment began in the Strathcona neighbourhood in the 1960s as several blocks of houses were razed to make way for public housing projects. During the next few years thousands of residents were displaced from their homes. Then, in 1967, the city revealed plans to build an eight-lane elevated freeway through Chinatown to the waterfront as part of a plan to link the harbour to the Trans-Canada Highway where it entered the city on the east. The proposed expressway would have destroyed a wide swath of the historic Chinese community as well as much of the area to the north, skid road. At about the same time, Canadian Pacific announced Project 200, a huge redevelopment scheme along the waterfront that would have destroyed most of Gastown.

While the partial destruction of Strathcona had been accepted by the rest of the city, the freeway scheme and Project 200 were met with an unprecedented level of opposition from the community. In Gastown, business interests joined with heritage activists to convince city officials not to endorse Project 200. Instead, a process of gentrification took place by which older buildings were renovated and new businesses were established. Gastown emerged from this makeover as a trendy tourist destination, minus many low-income residents who had been forced to move elsewhere. Meanwhile, an alliance of community groups, including Chinese Canadians, social activists, academics, heritage preservationists and some members of the business community succeeded in halting the freeway project.

Heartened by this experience, Chinatown's leaders renewed their efforts to stop the ongoing razing of Strathcona and succeeded in convincing all levels of government that the future of the neighbourhood lay in preservation and rehabilitation, not destruction.

Out of all this activism was born, in 1973, the Downtown Eastside Residents Association (DERA), which began to speak for the residents of this neglected neighbourhood. During this period of unprecedented civic activism, skid road was rebranded as the Downtown Eastside, a community where people lived instead of a blighted urban core. No one denied that the area faced serious problems of poverty, drug use and crime, but these became issues to address instead of conditions to deplore and ignore. John Turvey explained the difference:

> Skid Road is a mythology. Don't be fooled by it. A mythology is a thing people create because it allows them a place to come from; it makes it easier to deal with a situation. It can also mean you can come down here and abuse the situation or not relate to anybody as a real person. So if you call this place Skid Road, you create those attitudes. But if you call it a community and start perceiving it that way, talking about the dimensions of it, that it's a community that nurtures and feeds and cares for itself, then all of a sudden you're conveying to the rest of the city and the province that it has all the dimensions of any community.[13]

At about the same time, Chinatown also enjoyed an image makeover. For decades outsiders had seen the area as a centre of criminal vice and moral depravity, but by the 1960s such attitudes were moderating. Instead of a ghetto, Chinatown was seen as a colourful ethnic neighbourhood. With the easing of immigration restrictions following the Second World War, Canada had opened its door to people from a wide variety of places that had once been considered unacceptable sources of newcomers, such as the Caribbean,

East and South Asia and Africa. To go along with the new hetero-
geneity of its population, the country adopted a new ideology, mul-
ticulturalism, expressed as official government policy by Prime
Minister Pierre Trudeau in 1971. The transformation of Chinatown
was part of the general trend towards celebrating the ethnocultural
mosaic. The Chinese population of the city doubled between 1951
and 1961 (to 15,223), then doubled again during the next ten years.
By no means all of these people lived in or near Chinatown, but the
neighbourhood remained the focus of their community. Instead of
being fearful and suspicious, outsiders were now attracted to the
busy streets to sample their exotic otherness. Historic buildings were
preserved, streetscapes received a facelift, new attractions were
added, and Chinatown became one of the city's popular tourist destinations. In discussions of prostitution, the neighbourhood was no
longer singled out for particular mention. Or, more accurately, it
was subsumed under the more general category of the Downtown
Eastside.

As far as prostitution was concerned, Vancouver during the 1960s
experienced a lull before the storm. Women continued to conduct
their business on the city's streets and in its bars and hotels, but for
a while at least the public and the politicians seemed to have
exhausted their moral outrage. John Lowman has pointed out that
Vancouver newspapers paid relatively little attention to the issue in
this period.[14] Police continued to regulate and prosecute prostitutes
but they did not mount any campaigns to drive them from the
streets, and there was no organized public demand that they do so.

Nor was there much concern about the proliferation of body rub parlours and escort agencies that provided thin cover for sex workers.

To the extent that there was a greater public tolerance of commercial sex, some of the change surely had to do with the new permissiveness associated with the counterculture of the period. By the mid-sixties the baby boom generation had embarked on an era of sex, drugs and rock 'n' roll. Everything seemed possible; anything was allowed. The birth control pill, approved for sale in Canada in 1961, appeared to take the risk out of premarital sex. AIDS was still in the future; the development of antibiotics had made venereal disease less of a danger than it had ever been. The conventional restraints on sexual conduct were relaxed.

The 1960s was a decade of isms: nationalism, environmentalism, separatism—in Quebec, even terrorism. Of all the isms the one that had the biggest impact on attitudes towards prostitution was feminism. The women's movement was divided on the issue of commercial sex. Some leaders of the movement did not consider prostitution even to be a feminist issue. Among those who did, some thought of prostitutes as victims, exploited by male pimps and customers and a patriarchal society that viewed all women as sex objects. They argued that the existence of prostitution was harmful to all women and that it should be abolished. Other members of the women's movement preferred to think of prostitutes as independent businesswomen who chose the life they led. One sociologist, Deborah Brock, expressed this viewpoint in a book she wrote on the subject. "The labelling of the prostitute as 'victim' is an affront to the many assertive, independent, adult women who state that they would not subject themselves to the more 'respectable' female job ghetto," she wrote. "It ignores the fact that they may regard their jobs as a form of self-empowerment that provides them with a degree of financial well-being, and therefore more control over their own lives."[15] Either way, most feminists were unhappy with a law that seemed to victimize female prostitutes while ignoring the part played by their male customers.

In 1967, in response to lobbying by women's groups across the country, Prime Minister Lester Pearson's Liberal government had appointed a Royal commission to investigate the status of women in Canadian society. The commission, chaired by an Ottawa journalist, Florence Bird, was not mandated to study prostitution in particular, but its final report, issued in 1970, led to significant changes in the Criminal Code. Accepting the principle that men and women should be equal under the law, the commissioners noted that the vagrancy provisions of the Code applied only to women. They also pointed out that vagrancy of this type was a so-called status offence; that is, "prostitutes are charged not for what they do but for what they are considered to be."[16] Commissioners agreed with witnesses who argued that prostitution was a social problem, not a criminal one, and that a criminal record and/or a jail term made it that much more difficult for a woman to leave the profession. The report recommended that the vagrancy provision of the Criminal Code as it pertained to prostitution should be repealed. It also recommended that vagrancy as a whole no longer be an offence since "vagrants are not criminals".[17]

The Bird Commission was not alone in noting the inequity of Vag. C. It joined a chorus of complaints from civil libertarians and women's groups that politicians found impossible to ignore. As a result, in July 1972 the federal government repealed the vagrancy section of the Criminal Code and replaced it with Section 195.1, which made it illegal to solicit someone in a public place for the purpose of prostitution. Both men and women were covered by the new statute. The act of prostitution remained legal; it was the soliciting of clients that became the offence. As we shall see, the definition of *soliciting* kept lawyers, police and prostitutes searching their dictionaries for the next fifteen years.

※ ※ ※

For decades prostitution had been an issue for the east side of the city where, for the most part, police and civic officials were happy to confine it. During the 1970s this changed, and the west side of the downtown peninsula became the focus of the most heated debates. Of course, there had always been working women active on the west side, in various nightclubs, for example, or along the Granville Street theatre strip. But for the most part they worked indoors and didn't draw a lot of attention to themselves.

During the middle years of the decade, a period in which prostitution, and especially street prostitution, seemed to be on the increase, authorities received two reports that gave a comprehensive assessment of the scope of such activity in Vancouver. The first was prepared for the provincial police commission by Monique Layton, a graduate student in anthropology at the University of British Columbia. Originally Mrs. Layton had intended to assess the extent of juvenile prostitution in the city, but she expanded her parameters to include commercial sex of all types, including male prostitution, which had become a visible factor for the first time. Her report was made public in September 1975. The second study, dated September 1977, was conducted by a police corporal, G.A. Forbes, and was concerned particularly with the perceived increase in street prostitution in the city's West End.

The reports showed that street prostitution was localized in five main downtown neighbourhoods. The first was the area east of Main Street in Strathcona on either side of East Hastings, what Layton called skid row. The second was slightly to the west, in the blocks surrounding Hastings and Columbia. Both these neighbourhoods were part of what had become the Downtown Eastside; they had been centres of commercial sex from the city's earliest days. Three other locations were on the west side of downtown, an area that traditionally police had tried to keep clear of visible prostitution. One was along Granville Street, roughly between Georgia and Davie. Another surrounded the intersection of Georgia and Hornby where there were large hotels such as the Hotel Vancouver, the Hotel Georgia and the Devonshire Hotel, and several night clubs. Finally, Davie Street from Thurlow westward towards Denman had emerged during the early part of the decade as a busy stroll for both male and female prostitutes. It was this West End neighbourhood that became the focus of much of the debate about prostitution in the city during the seventies and early eighties.

Layton estimated that there were about 300 female prostitutes in the city, a figure that included "streetwalkers" and women working out of bars and nightclubs.[18] Forbes thought there were anywhere from 500 to 650, of which he classified 350 as street prostitutes.[19] The rest worked off-street out of hotels, nightclubs, bars and body-rub parlours or as part of call-girl operations. (An even higher estimate of the number of "working girls" was given by Vic Lake, head of the police vice squad, who told the *Sun* that in the summertime there were about 2,000 prostitutes in the city, "varying from the Skid

Road variety to the beautiful girls who hang out in the downtown hotels and nightclubs."[20]

While Layton found that some girls were as young as fourteen, she estimated that most street prostitutes were between eighteen and twenty-one years old. The majority worked for a pimp who was often a boyfriend or husband. Layton drew special attention to the role of black pimps.[21] A disproportionate number of pimps were black compared to the relatively small number of people of African descent living in the city. The police counted more than one hundred black pimps, with their number increasing during the summer. Some were locals; many were Americans who carried on business between Vancouver and the United States. The retired police officer Bill Harkema remembered that many were armed forces personnel from the American base on Whidbey Island in Washington.[22] The Stratford Hotel pub at Keefer and Gore was a well-known hangout. Prostitution was, and still is, a highly mobile profession, with women being moved around a circuit that included cities in Alberta and along the West Coast down to California. In July 1976, the *Sun* reported an "invasion" of African-American pimps from south of the border. According to the paper, these men visited the city during the summer and attempted to steal women from local pimps. Supposedly they were more violent than the locals, beating women in order to terrorize them into doing as they were told. The article estimated that between 150 and 200 pimps, both outsiders and locals, were in the city.[23]

The phenomenon was not new. Robert Welsh, who worked as a detective on the city's morality squad in the mid-1960s, described "an extensive ring of black pimps" operating out of Seattle and Los Angeles.

They covered a lot of territory, trying to recruit girls they met in nightclubs up and down the Coast and far inland. The recruiter was usually quite a swinger, a good dancer with lots of money to spend and recent Cadillac to drive. They would use the older girls to start a young one turning tricks. The newcomer would become the number two or three girl. The pimp's number one girl controlled the others. If any of them got out of line, she and the pimp would beat the hell out of them.[24]

Police sometimes used unorthodox methods to intimidate these American pimps into leaving the city. Welsh records an occasion when he brought one of them in for questioning and another officer, the head of the morality squad, walked into the interview room wearing a Ku Klux Klan robe and hood. "Not approved procedure," Welsh admitted, "but it sure worked well."[25]

According to Layton, the relationships were not always as coercive as the press and police implied. Some women were attracted to African-American pimps because they seemed exotic, dressing smartly and conveying by their language and manner a hip, urban coolness. "Unsophisticated Canadian girls, especially from small towns, often find such an appeal irresistible," Layton observed. Furthermore, many of the women were defiant towards family and authority, and for them an African-American pimp/boyfriend was the ultimate act of rebellion. "Whereas it is a damaging mistake to see a pimp in every black man," Layton concluded, "I also think it is a serious mistake to underestimate the *mystique* of black pimping."[26] She also might have pointed out that although some pimps were blacks, almost all johns were white.

According to Corporal Forbes, there was a hierarchy involved in the distribution of street prostitution. "The highest class of street prostitute" worked the Georgia Street area, charging between $50 and $100 a trick. They catered to men who were staying at hotels or who were nightclub patrons. Women working on Davie Street were slightly less expensive; most of their customers arrived by car, and dates occurred in nearby parking lots and alleyways. On the Granville Street strip, women used "hot sheet" hotels that offered rooms for half an hour at $3 to $5. "Many women have mentioned to me that these smaller hotels offer their only protection," wrote Layton. "The man at the desk will watch the time and knock on the door if he feels they have been there too long. They give him an extra $2 or so, but feel it is well worth it."[27] Drugs by this time were fuelling prostitution, particularly heroin. "Drugs, whether cause or result, go hand in hand with prostitution," noted Layton, who estimated that one half of the women were addicted, along with their pimps.[28] Drugs were part of the hierarchy. Forbes thought that by and large the Georgia and Davie street strolls were drug-free and the women there looked down on the Granville Street and East End prostitutes who were considered to be heavy drug users willing to turn a trick for the cost of a cap of heroin (about $35 in the mid-1970s).[29] Layton identified another group of prostitutes who worked the waterfront bars that catered to sailors off visiting freighters. "Most of the shipping companies have standing orders not to allow these girls on board, but a blind eye is often seen as the best policy to keep the crew fairly satisfied," she wrote.[30]

Along with female prostitutes, there were also between 150 and 200 male prostitutes working in the city. According to Forbes, this number had increased noticeably since the beginning of the decade. Ranging in age from fourteen to their mid-twenties, they frequented the same Davie and Granville street strolls as the women and also worked out of steam baths, bars and clubs. Forbes believed that the majority of male hustlers were juveniles who did not have pimps. "Usually twenty-five to thirty hard core regulars make themselves available on Davie Street, from Thurlow to Denman, including English Bay and the Bath House at English Bay. Young male prostitutes can be seen in small groups on corners, seated at bus benches or associating with female prostitutes on either side of Davie Street."[31] They were routinely harassed by homophobes who hurled insults, and bottles, from passing cars. Forbes also reported that about twenty transvestites worked the Davie stroll.

❋ ❋ ❋

In her report, Monique Layton paid special attention to the Penthouse Cabaret, a notorious Seymour Street nightspot. Its owner, Joe Philliponi, had bought the site along with his brothers in 1938 (and moved into a suite of rooms next door). There the family operated a string of businesses, including a delivery service and the Diamond Cab Company, though during the war the brothers ran a steak house and an athletic club and in the fifties expanded the operation into a full-fledged nightclub. Before it received a liquor licence, the Penthouse was a bottle club where patrons served themselves discreetly from illegal bottles concealed under the table. It was a popular hangout with entertainers, newspaper types and hangers-on who wanted a late-night drink, a bite to eat and a chance to catch sight of a visiting show-biz celebrity. Harry Belafonte, Sammy Davis Jr., Ella Fitzgerald, Louis Armstrong and many other top talents played the Penthouse. The actor Errol Flynn dropped in the night before he died at a West End apartment in the arms of his seventeen-year-old girlfriend. In those days police routinely raided the place for liquor infractions. "We used to have spotters on the roof," recalled one of the brothers, Ross Filippone (those born in Canada spelled the name differently). "You couldn't miss five or six police cars coming down the street. We'd press a buzzer and tell the waiters, who'd tell the customers [to hide their bottles]. It was a joke."[32] Joe Philliponi was a bit of a local celebrity himself, known for his outspoken turn of phrase and a personal flair for fashion. One newspaper reporter described him as "shaped like an egg: small, round and smooth. A garnished egg, because Joe's wardrobe—orange shirt, brown checked jacket, green plaid pants and patterned tie—looks as if it was pulled at random out of a spin dryer."[33]

By the 1960s, Philliponi's club was a flourishing centre of prostitution. As Layton reported, "its reputation extends throughout Canada, and even beyond." As many as a hundred women worked out of the club every evening. It was a convenient and safe place to meet customers and make dates, and various people profited from the setup. A prostitute entering the club paid a $2.95 cover charge, more if she were returning after a trick, plus a $2 tip for the doorman and the maitre d'. She sat at a reserved table, for which she tipped the hostess $2. Other tips were paid to anyone who sent a customer her way. The club made cash advances available to patrons wishing to use their credit cards to pay for a prostitute, at a twenty percent surcharge. Taxis lined up three deep on the street to carry the women and their customers to the nearby hotels. In the unlikely event of a police raid, the women were alerted by an announcement over the public address system, "Mrs. Finley has arrived". When management spotted a woman talking to an undercover cop she had not recognized, she was called away to the telephone.[34]

The police, some of whom were regular visitors, knew full well what was going on at the Penthouse and other clubs like it; for the most part they tolerated it as a nuisance-free alternative to street-walking. Then, in December 1975, police raided the Penthouse and a second club, the Zanzibar. Why authorities decided to shut down the clubs at this particular time, when prostitutes had been working there for so long, is not clear. As the *Sun* columnist Allan Fotheringham pointed out, "The hooker shop known as the Penthouse has been existing for decades. It has been known as one of the landmarks of the town, a minor league equivalent of the Eiffel Tower and the Empire State Building."[35] The bust may have been connected to Layton's report, made public three months earlier, but Fotheringham believed it had to do with the arrival of a new police chief, Don Winterton, "a squeaky-clean guy with a new broom" who wanted to show that he meant business about cleaning up vice. Joe Philliponi attributed the raid to a feud he had with the new head of the vice squad, Vic Lake. This version of events is confirmed by Bill Harkema, who recalls that Lake, who had strong feelings against prostitutes anyway, was angry at Philliponi for suddenly refusing to allow police officers to hang out in the club.[36] Whatever the reason, the police launched an investigation, using photographic surveillance and a young female constable posing as a prostitute; they also taped conversations with Joe's brother Ross. Satisfied they had the evidence they needed, authorities laid charges against Joe Philliponi, his brothers Ross and Mickey Filippone, a doorman and two cashiers, alleging conspiracy to live off the avails of prostitution, corrupting public morals and keeping a common bawdy house, as well as bookmaking and recording bets. (As for the Zanzibar, the case never came to trial. The club burned down, and though the owner was charged with arson he was not convicted.)

During the Penthouse trial, which began in September 1976 and was not concluded until March of the following year, the Crown alleged that the club used the presence of prostitutes as a drawing card to attract customers and made money from the operations of the women who did business on the premises. Lawyers for the Penthouse argued that the owners could hardly be held responsible for everything that went on in their club, and pointed out that the women did not share their proceeds with management or turn tricks on the premises. The trial continued for sixty-one court days and featured sometimes sensational testimony that kept the city mesmerized. It was dubbed the "Charge-sex trial" after the Chargex credit cards that many patrons used to buy sex. One prostitute appeared on the witness stand disguised in a wig and dark glasses and refused to identify her pimp, who was sitting in the courtroom, for fear she would be beaten. A pair of schoolgirls told the court how they had visited the Penthouse hoping to turn a trick. A fresh-faced police recruit named Leslie Schulze had her picture splashed across the front pages when she recounted her activities posing as a prostitute in the cabaret. At one point a genuine seventeen-year-old prostitute told how she had had to pass a test before being allowed to use the club; she had to give Ross Filippone oral sex, she said. Later Filippone's lawyer introduced physical evidence to prove that the woman was unfamiliar with his client's penis. "If she did perform an oral sex act," he told the court, "it certainly was not on Ross Filippone."[37]

In his own defence, Joe Philliponi compared the Penthouse to a lonely hearts' club. "It was just a question of boy meets girl", he told Judge William Trainor with a straight face.[38] But the judge found five of the defendants guilty of conspiring to live off the avails (Mickey got off), fined them, and sentenced Joe and Ross to sixty days in jail as well. In December, however, the BC Court of Appeal overturned the convictions. After a brief argument with the civic government over renewing its licence (at one point Joe accused city council of Nazi tactics) the Penthouse reopened, though its days as a celebrity-filled nightspot were over. The club turned to exotic dancers, a polite term for strippers, though eventually the prostitutes returned to do business there. The police undercover operation and the legal proceedings had cost taxpayers $2 million.

Ironically, it was not long before authorities realized that they had made a mistake by raiding the Penthouse. During the next decade, as the situation on the streets deteriorated, many people looked back at Philliponi's club as representing a sensible, if partial, answer to the problems associated with prostitution. In 1983 one West End prostitute expressed this point of view when interviewed by a researcher.

You know what I thought was a really good idea, the Penthouse. The girls were off the streets. They didn't have to worry about meeting customers. Customers were screened when they went into the Penthouse. If there was a weirdo, the bouncers at the Penthouse would protect you. The Penthouse was a good place. It really was. Everyone knew prostitutes were there. There were cops in there all the time but who cares about them. Mainly they were there for customers who were being ripped off and as soon as they found out in the Penthouse that you're ripping someone off, you didn't work there anymore, or if you had a disease, you didn't work there any-more. It was controlled. It was really a good place...[39]

A footnote to the Penthouse story occurred on the evening of 18 September 1983 when Joe Philliponi was murdered in the office of his home adjoining the club. Shortly after seeing his ninety-two-year-old mother to bed, Philliponi had met with Scott Forsyth, a twenty-five-year-old unemployed painter from Ontario, ostensibly to take delivery of some plumbing supplies. Forsyth forced the club owner at gunpoint to open his safe, then shot him once through the head. Forsyth was arrested at Exhibition Park race track a few days later. While in jail he confessed to an undercover police officer planted in the cell with him. Faced with his own confession, Forsyth implicated a second man, Sid Morrisroe, a Burnaby plumber and former boxer. According to Forsyth, Morrisroe had come up with the plan to rob and kill Philliponi, but had backed out at the last moment. Directly after the murder Forsyth went to a Burnaby motor hotel where he met Morrisroe in the bar and the two men split the $1,200 taken from the safe. In June 1984 a jury convicted Forsyth and Morrisroe of first-degree murder, and they were sentenced to life in prison with no parole for twenty-five years. Morrisroe, who always maintained his innocence, claiming he was framed, received early parole in 2002. He was sixty-eight years old and suffered from serious health problems.[40] In 2006, the Penthouse, a notorious part of the city's nightlife for more than half a century, was slated for demolition to make way for a condominium tower.

Four

THERE OUGHT TO BE A LAW

The Penthouse affair was important not just for what it revealed about the operations of prostitutes in the city but also for the impact it had on the subsequent evolution of the sex "industry". Other clubs, fearful of prosecution, told their in-house prostitutes to take their business somewhere else. Hundreds of women lost their principal place of employment. As a result they spilled back out onto the streets, jostling for business with other women already working there. The strolls located on the west side of the downtown caused particular concern with authorities, and with the public, because they were outside the traditional neighbourhoods where prostitution had long been tolerated. At about the same time, in 1977, there was a cross-Canada crackdown on massage parlours. Police raided these establishments in major cities and charged the women with being inmates of common bawdy houses, disrupting yet another venue where prostitutes could work away from the street. As John Lowman has pointed out, there were still other reasons for the apparent rise in street prostitution. Drug use, especially of heroin, was increasing in the city, and clubs that had tolerated the presence of working women did not want drugs on their premises. Nor did the club owners wish to put up with the growing number of prostitutes under eighteen years of age who worked the streets as well as the clubs. For a variety of reasons, then, more women were moving their business onto the downtown strolls.[1]

The solicitation law passed in 1972 was difficult to enforce, in part because the definition of soliciting was unclear. Prostitution itself was not illegal, whereas the solicitation of customers in a public place was. The law was silent on the twin questions of what constituted a public place and what kind of behaviour constituted soliciting. Matters became even more ambiguous in spring 1978 when the Supreme Court of Canada submitted its ruling in the case of *R. v. Hutt*. Debra Hutt was a Vancouver prostitute who had been arrested in May 1975 for offering to perform oral sex on an undercover police detective at the Dufferin Hotel. She was convicted of soliciting but fought the verdict all the way to the Supreme Court, which eventually ruled that the behaviour of a soliciting prostitute had to be "pressing and persistent" in order for it to be illegal. Basically, the court argued "no harm, no foul". If a prostitute was not being a nuisance by aggressively selling him or herself, then police had no case. (The court also commented that a car, which was where Hutt and her detective conducted their negotiations, was not a public place, though this was not the issue being adjudicated.) Hutt's conviction was struck down, much to the consternation of Mayor Jack Volrich and the Vancouver police who together had been conducting a war on vice during the winter of 1977–78, with a special police task force, organized in September 1977, busily arresting hundreds of prostitutes and charging them with soliciting. The Hutt decision nullified all this industrious street-sweeping. When was behaviour "pressing and persistent"? Since police could not be sure, they more or less gave up charging offenders with soliciting. In all of 1978, Vancouver police laid a mere sixty-eight soliciting charges.[2]

Street prostitution had been increasing as a neighbourhood nuisance; following the Hutt decision, police, the press and local politicians, led by a crusading Mayor Volrich, perceived it to be a "crisis". Attention focused mainly on two areas: the corner of Georgia and Hornby and the West End, specifically Davie Street.

For years prostitutes had been present at the former location, working discreetly and in small numbers, catering mainly to men staying in nearby hotels. With the closure of the Penthouse, the number of women working in this area escalated sharply. Hotel operators began to complain that their patrons were being accosted in the street. At one point the general manager of the Devonshire Hotel closed the dining room at six p.m. because diners were offended by the sex traffic outside. As the press began labelling the city "the hooker capital of North America" and "a hooker's paradise", the downtown business community grew alarmed at the possible impact on tourism. The situation seemed to grow worse following the Hutt decision when prostitutes were emboldened to defy police. "The flaunting of their wares has become much less furtive", wrote a reporter in the *Globe and Mail.* "They're moving from the dingier, more shadowy areas on the fringes of downtown into the neon glare of some of the city's prominent squares and intersections." In the spring of 1979, police launched a campaign to rid the area of prostitutes. By the end of the year they had succeeded, but only temporarily. Two years later the *Province* was reporting that the corner was once again "a high-priced hooker heaven" where as many as forty women a night met their dates.[3]

On Davie Street the situation was complicated by the fact that the stroll was in the middle of a residential neighbourhood. Prostitutes, male and female, began appearing along this West End street at least as early as 1972, but the number climbed with the closure of the Penthouse. At the same time, the area was going through a process of gentrification as older rooming houses and low-rise apartments were replaced or renovated and a forest of high-rises appeared. As the tone and the income level of the neighbourhood rose, residents grew less tolerant of prostitutes in their midst. Nick Larsen argues that another factor was an informal "hands off" policy on the part of the police who, by claiming they were hamstrung by the Hutt decision, hoped to increase public pressure in favour of stiffer anti-prostitution laws.[4]

West End residents argued that their streets no longer belonged to them but had been taken over by an occupying army of prostitutes, pimps and thugs. Women and young men were turning tricks in cars on side streets, in back alleys and in parking lots and underground parkades. Prostitutes began work early in the morning to catch commuters and stayed at work late into the night, causing traffic congestion and keeping the residents awake. Women were reportedly harassed in the street and pedestrians bullied on the sidewalks, which were littered with used condoms. Especially troubling to the public were reports of the increased incidence of boys under the age of sixteen working the stroll. In an article in the *Province*, one reporter, Marcus Gee, painted a lurid picture of young men, termed "chickens", turning tricks for $30 or $40 and sometimes posing for pornographic movies as well. Gee raised the spectre of youngsters being kidnapped off the streets of Vancouver and "shipped to homosexuals" in New York and Los Angeles. In 1977, police warned that it was only a matter of time before Davie Street saw a gruesome murder similar to the one that had occurred in Toronto when a twelve-year-old shoeshine boy named Emanuel Jacques died "after a homosexual orgy" on the Yonge Street strip.[5] Reports such as this one made clear that Vancouverites were working themselves up into a full blown moral panic. And they knew who to blame: the courts, which had left police powerless to deal with the situation, and the politicians who were refusing to fix the law. Such was the view of the *Sun* columnist Denny Boyd. Describing a drive down Davie Street, Boyd wrote:

> I see the ugliest side of the whole prostitute syndrome. The 17-year-old girls, wobbling on high heels they haven't learned to control yet; the boys in the silver bomber jackets, working the pavement shadows at Davie and Broughton [...] As a citizen of this city I am tired of having Georgia Street taken away from me, fed up to the gills with having Davie Street turned into an avenue of squandered young lives. There is a sleaziness growing in this town where I live [...] It is here because there are fools in our high courts and moral hypocrites in our governments.[6]

Mayor Volrich, impatient at the lack of action by federal politicians, threatened to enact new civic bylaws to sweep the prostitutes from the street, and Police Chief Don Winterton admitted that "there's been no problem more frustrating to me than prostitution".[7]

✳ ✳ ✳

As concern about street prostitution grew, a scandal broke that offered a glimpse into the usually shuttered world of the high-end off-street prostitute. In November 1978, right in the middle of the public uproar about prostitution, the chief justice of the BC Supreme Court, John Farris, suddenly announced that he was resigning from the bench. His decision took everyone by surprise, but his name was soon linked in the press with a thirty-year-old West End call girl named Wendy King who was arrested a short time later. Police had had King under surveillance for several months as part of a narcotics investigation. They had tapped her telephone and recorded more than three hundred conversations, two of which, it turned out, were with Farris who was calling to make dates to see her. He was also photographed arriving at King's apartment. When police later raided the apartment they found no drugs but they did find a "little brown notebook" containing the names of eight hundred persons, most of them clients, some of them socially and politically prominent. An informant whose identity was never revealed leaked the fact that Farris was involved in the King affair. The judge's resignation came after he learned that the Judicial Council of Canada was looking into the matter, whereupon the council cut short its investigation. King eventually pleaded guilty to charges of keeping a bawdy house, so the public was denied the pleasure of a prolonged trial with testimony from some of the prostitute's supposedly illustrious clientele. She received a nine-month probationary sentence and had to pay a fine of $1,500. The court ordered the infamous "trick book" and the transcripts of the phone taps sealed, their contents never to be made public.[8]

Two years later, at the end of 1980, the scandal resurfaced with the publication of *The Wendy King Story*, a book written by Robert Wilson in collaboration with King, with an introduction by the broadcaster Laurier LaPierre. The book presented King as "an open-minded flower child of the '60s" who drifted into prostitution in the early 1970s after dropping out of university. She was attracted to prostitution by the independent lifestyle it seemed to offer. She saw it, however, not only as an easy way to make money without being tied to a nine-to-five job, but also as "an act of defiance against what the establishment stood for". She went to work for a friend who ran a call-girl operation where her clients were mainly "upper middle class, white-collar men" whom she entertained in her apartment, where they chatted and shared drinks. Sometimes they went out to restaurants or nightclubs. As King was the first to admit, this was a far cry from the furtive encounters of the street prostitute. She considered herself a kind of sex counsellor, and the book argued that prostitution served a socially useful purpose and should be legalized.[9]

The Wendy King Story contained transcripts of the taped telephone conversations with Farris, as well as another bombshell. King claimed that her client list included a second prominent jurist, whom she identified as "Davey F".[10] Readers had little difficulty supposing that "Davey F" was E. Davie Fulton, a former federal cabinet minister in John Diefenbaker's government and himself a judge on the BC Supreme Court. When the book appeared, Fulton sued the author and publisher for libel, and his lawyer, Peter Butler, sent a letter to bookstores threatening to include them in the court action if they did not remove the book from their shelves. When the stores complied, the publisher, Ron Langen, opened the Wendy King Book Store in the heart of the Davie Street stroll where customers could buy an autographed copy for $14.95.[11] Eventually King publicly apologized to Fulton, admitting in court that she had never met him.

At the national level, the government was hearing more and more complaints about the inadequacy of the legislation related to prostitution. Not sure what to do, and reluctant to do anything, Ottawa convened the Special Committee on Pornography and Prostitution, a panel of seven legal experts who were asked to provide the minister of justice with an analysis of the problems associated with these two areas of public policy. The committee, chaired by Paul Fraser, a Vancouver lawyer, held public hearings across the country during the first six months of 1984. In Vancouver, the creation of the committee was met with angry impatience. Mayor Mike Harcourt called it a waste of time and accused the Liberal government of using the committee as a stalling tactic. What Harcourt wanted was a change to the solicitation law that would allow police to get hookers off the streets. The provincial attorney general, Brian Smith, echoed the mayor's complaints, calling the Fraser committee an "outrageous" misuse of time and money. In the *Sun*, Denny Boyd managed to frame the issue as a regional grievance. He charged that the federal Liberals were refusing to act on prostitution because they were afraid of alienating the "Canada-wide feminist vote". "The Liberals would rather be damned regionally for what they do not do than be damned nationally for what they do," he wrote.[12]

As part of its investigation, the Fraser Committee commissioned studies of prostitution in several major cities. The Vancouver one was carried out by a team led by Simon Fraser University criminologist John Lowman. His report contained statistics showing the steady decline in the number of prostitution-related offences since the mid-1970s and pointed out that this decline predated the decision in *R. v Hutt*. In other words, despite the claims of the press and the police, the soliciting law had proven ineffective long before

Hutt. It was not the Supreme Court that was to blame for the problems on Vancouver streets. The Lowman study included the results of interviews with police officers, social agencies and the prostitutes themselves and gives probably the clearest portrait of the sex trade in the city yet produced.[13] It concluded that the most significant factor in persuading someone to become a prostitute was economic necessity. Recognizing that many, if not most, prostitutes came from dysfunctional families and were victims of physical and sexual abuse, the study argued that prostitution offered a lifestyle that seemed to provide financial independence. Many of the benefits turned out to be illusory, but by then the individual was entrenched in the life, possibly addicted to drugs or coerced by a pimp or both. The study also made the point that street prostitutes accounted for only a portion of the prostitution in the city, perhaps as little as twenty percent. The rest took place in massage and body rub parlours and through dating and escort services. This off-street part of the business had also increased significantly during the early 1980s.

On the streets, prostitutes tended to frequent the same neighbourhood day after day, though they shifted to another district, or another city, from time to time. Not surprisingly, prostitutes chose to work areas where it was easiest to "catch dates" and where friends were also working. Strolls were divided into areas according to the age and sex of the prostitutes. Teenage male hustlers might hang round one corner, transgendered ones round another, and so on. As one informant explained: "A territory is established by a person that's usually been there the longest and the new people that come on to that territory owe the person that has been there the longest a degree of respect for letting them come to work there because they're in the area where I'm going to make money so obviously they are going to affect my income." Newcomers had to be careful about insinuating themselves into a spot on the street and be ready to defend their patch. "When I went down there I had to stand up to everybody; it's a test of guts."[14]

Lowman and his researchers discovered that the role of the pimp was more problematic than expected. Certainly some of the women were controlled by pimps who took all or most of their income and often brutalized them. As one angry woman said: "Nothing can be done until you get the pimps off the bloody streets because the girls get beat up regularly, they have their money taken away from them, you've got to produce the money or else, and if you get caught keeping it, you get badly beaten. Whether he's black, white or yellow, it don't matter and in most cases it doesn't matter what their skin tone is, most of them are yellow anyway because they can't beat on a man, they have to beat up their bitches and that's all they're good for."[15] Most of the informants claimed to work independently of pimps. They may have had boyfriends with whom they lived and with whom they voluntarily shared their money, but they did not consider these men pimps. Almost all said that they had been assaulted, not by pimps but by customers. They reported being raped, beaten, robbed, threatened with guns and knives, run over by cars. One woman, an eight-year veteran of the streets, said she had been on "hundreds and hundreds of bad dates". The study concluded that "prostitution is an extremely dangerous profession" and that "prostitutes need protection".[16]

In mid-January 1984, Paul Fraser and his colleagues arrived in Vancouver for three days of public hearings. They heard from a variety of individuals and community groups, most of whom wanted to talk about the continuing deterioration of Davie Street. "Night after sleepless night, [we] suffer from a barrage of squealing tires, breaking bottles, screaming, laughing, cursing, crying", complained a brief from the West End Seniors Network. "What you see in the West End is the total disintegration of a neighbourhood", Pat Carney, the Conservative MP for Vancouver Centre, told the committee, at the same time calling the justice minister "weak-kneed and lily-livered" for not implementing stricter laws. Residents presented a study, later revealed to be based more on speculation than on solid research, blaming prostitution for a $14-million decline in West End land values. Legal counsel for the city, appearing along with Alderman May Brown, explained that city hall wanted the hookers off the street but didn't much mind if they continued to work the bars and nightclubs, admitting in hindsight that there was a link between the closing of the Penthouse in 1975, which the city now regretted, and the subsequent increase in street prostitution. The committee heard from some womens' groups who sympathized with the prostitutes. Most speakers, however, were angry at Ottawa's inaction and convinced that the police needed tougher laws to suppress prostitution.[17]

While Fraser and his committee continued to tour the country and write their report, matters escalated on Davie Street, where West Enders had become increasingly militant. Some residents had come together in late September 1981 to form CROWE, Concerned Residents of the West End, a vociferous lobby group whose chief concern was to rid the area of hookers, not to debate the niceties of prostitution law. Their quarrel, they said, was not with commercial sex but rather with all the nuisance activities that accompanied it: the noise, littering, intimidation and general crime that came with the transformation of their neighbourhood into an open-air sex bazaar. Members of CROWE were politically savvy, well organized and determined. They kept up a steady flow of petitions and research reports, documenting the deleterious impact of prostitution on the daily life of their neighbourhood. (Meanwhile, high-end prostitution continued to go on without any public complaint. For example, in February 1982, police raided a West End penthouse apartment where they found a dozen prostitutes operating a brothel masquerading as a modelling agency. Customers were described as "prominent Lower Mainland men". "It was a high-class operation," said one police officer, "and you have to live in the right neighbourhood to afford it."[18])

In April 1982, the civic government, impatient with the lack of direction from Ottawa, decided to take the Davie Street matter into its own hands by passing the Street Activities Bylaw, which made it an offence to buy or sell sexual services on the street. Police could issue summonses to prostitutes or their customers; on conviction, fines ranged from $350 to $2,000. Mayor Harcourt made it clear that the intention of the bylaw was not to eradicate prostitution but rather to push it indoors. "Be discreet, don't use the streets", he told the prostitutes.[19] On 26 April, "K. Fowler" became the first person to plead guilty under the new bylaw. He received a fine of $350 for accosting an undercover policewoman "working" a downtown street corner. But the conviction raised a contentious issue. Neither Fowler's full name, nor his address, nor his occupation were made public. In fact, as the city prosecutor, Roland Bouwman, admitted, "Fowler" might well have been an alias; no one had bothered to check. Bouwman revealed that the city's policy was not to make public the names of anyone charged under the bylaw so long as they pleaded guilty. Furthermore, the city made it as difficult as possible for reporters to discover when cases were appearing in court. As Harcourt confirmed, this unusual treatment of accused criminals was an attempt to avoid a showdown. Civic officials worried—for good reason as it turned out—that their bylaw would not stand up to a legal challenge; that it was, in other words, illegal. As a *Sun* reporter named Linda Hossie put it: "Since everyone agrees that the bylaw is legally dicey, one solution [...] is to bribe the johns with anonymity."[20]

Inevitably a legal challenge did come, as everyone expected it would. A freelance writer, Donald Woodbury, charged under the bylaw, hired a lawyer named Tony Serka to contend that the civic law was invalid because it invaded federal jurisdiction and violated the Charter of Rights and Freedoms. Serka, the same lawyer who had defended Debra Hutt in her landmark case before the Supreme Court, presented his arguments to Judge David Moffett of the provincial court who in mid-September refused to strike down the bylaw, ruling that it was protecting the people's right to use the streets freely and regulating the conduct of business, as municipalities had the power to do. But if this was a victory for the anti-prostitution forces, it was a short-lived one. Early in 1983 the federal Supreme Court ruled that a similar bylaw in Calgary was *ultra vires*. Rather than continue a losing battle, Vancouver's city council rescinded its bylaw and the Crown dropped all outstanding charges laid under it.

Mayor Harcourt vowed to continue the fight to "clean up" the West End, which he said was in danger of being "taken over" by hookers and their pimps, but he shifted his tactics to lobbying the federal government to make significant changes to the Criminal Code.[21] He was furious when, in June, the federal justice minister announced plans to make only minor adjustments to the Code while the Fraser Committee was carrying out its investigation. "It's cuckoo-land," said the mayor. "If we are not going to get the changes we asked for immediately, they should just fold up their tent and let the outlaws run the country." Harcourt blamed the "feminist lobby" for weakening Ottawa's reponse to what Vancouver civic politicians thought was a crisis. Gordon Price, the head of CROWE, called Mark MacGuigan, the justice minister, "the best friend the hookers and pimps have ever had" and warned that residents might resort to violence to protect their streets.[22] The situation was drawing national attention, including that of a pair of filmmakers, Janis Cole and Holly Dale, whose documentary, *Hookers on Davie*, made during 1983, offered a sympathetic look at the women who were working the West End streets.

Violence did not occur that summer, but it appeared to grow more likely early the next spring when activist elements in the West End began engaging in an activity they called "Shaming the Johns". Groups of residents gathered round prostitutes on the sidewalks to discourage clients from approaching them, and took obvious note of automobiles that were cruising the streets, even photographing johns and copying down licence numbers, which they published. Not surprisingly, such tactics led to noisy confrontations involving pimps, prostitutes, customers and protestors. The likelihood of violence finally led the provincial government to intervene. In June, the provincial attorney general, Brian Smith, asked the BC Supreme Court to crack down on prostitutes in the West End. For the benefit of the judges, a government lawyer, Jack Giles, described "a sordid sex scene" in the environs of Davie Street where "church-going families" had to pick their way through used condoms, be assailed by foul language and witness "sidewalk fornication". Daily life had become intolerable for residents, Giles claimed.[23] The prostitutes presented their side of the case as well, but the court agreed with the residents. Chief Justice Allan McEachern called what was happening in the West End "an urban tragedy" and on 5 July issued an injunction banning prostitutes from the area west of Granville Street. Anyone violating the injunction could be arrested and charged with contempt of court. Members of CROWE held a party to celebrate the reclamation of their neighbourhood, but the court's decision was no victory for the city as a whole. The prostitutes simply relocated to other streets, as they had always done.

❋ ❋ ❋

In spring 1985 the Fraser Committee released its much-anticipated report. It tried to address the concerns of people in large cities whose neighbourhoods were being affected by the nuisances that accompanied street prostitution. At the same time, Fraser and his colleagues expressed sympathy for the prostitutes themselves, whom the report characterized as economically disadvantaged, often the victims of sexual abuse in the family, brutalized by pimps, at risk from customers. "Prostitutes agree that life on the street is a 'hell hole'," said the report. "Virtually all women prostitutes have been sexually assaulted, and some of them as often as three or four times a year; pimps are violent towards their prostitutes and prostitutes are violent towards each other. The competition to be on the street to earn some money is fierce. And [...] very little attention is paid to their specific needs in relation to social services."[24] Fraser argued that the law as it stood was useless. Pimps were seldom prosecuted. Operators of massage and body-rub parlours, the principal venues for indoor prostitution, had no trouble avoiding the bawdy house provisions of the Criminal Code. Police believed themselves to be powerless to halt the spread of street soliciting (though Fraser argued that this dissatisfaction with the law predated the infamous Supreme Court decision in *R. v Hutt*, which it had become conventional wisdom to blame for everything that was wrong with prostitution enforcement in the country). About the solicitation law, the report concluded: "With judges who appear to be reticent about convicting under it, law enforcement officials who are unwilling to use it, and a public who have been persuaded that it is useless, it is difficult to see how it can be infused with new life in its present form."[25]

Fraser warned that the desire to clean up the nuisance aspects of prostitution should not be coloured by "a certain nostalgia for 'the good old days'" when police could sweep up prostitutes as vagrants. Conversely, the report was also leery of proposals to decriminalize the sex business altogether or to allow it to operate in licensed brothels or government-regulated red light districts. In the end, the committee came down somewhere in the middle. Given that prostitution arose from economic factors, governments should dedicate themselves to ameliorating the inequalities between men and women in the workplace and in society at large. Also, there should be more and better sex education in the schools and more programmes to assist prostitutes needing health care and counselling. Turning to the law, the committee argued strenuously against repressive legislation. Quite the reverse, it suggested that any adult wishing to pursue the "lifestyle" should be free to do so, "with dignity and without harassment." On the issue of pimping, the committee thought that the law had to protect prostitutes from force or coercion, but also that adults were capable of making their own decisions about whether to enter, and remain in, "the life". And if a woman was in a relationship where she agreed to prostitute herself "to contribute to the family budget", this was no concern of the law.

One of the committee's guiding principles was that prostitution should take place in private "and without the opportunities for exploitation which have been traditionally associated with [it]". Therefore the report proposed changes to the bawdy house provisions of the Criminal Code to allow "regulated prostitution establishments", small-scale, non-residential operations (i.e., not brothels) where women at least nineteen years old could work free of intimidation in circumstances regulated by provincial labour codes and health standards. One change that the committee did recommend to aid police was that the legal definition of the term "public place" be expanded to include the inside of automobiles.[26]

The Fraser Report's liberalizing flavour did not go so far in the direction of decriminalization as some women's groups wished. Neither did it endorse the get-tough strategies that police and civic officials advocated. Rather, it presented a clear rationale for a radical new direction in public policy. While the committee had been holding hearings and writing its report, however, Brian Mulroney's Conservative government had replaced the Liberals in Ottawa and the new government was unsympathetic to the liberal spirit of Fraser and his colleagues. The Conservatives decided to give the police what they wanted, and at the end of 1985 Justice Minister John Crosbie introduced Bill C-49, repealing the soliciting law. No longer would it be necessary for prostitutes to be "pressing and persistent" in their behaviour. Instead, according to a new section (213.1) of the Criminal Code, communication between a prostitute and a potential client "for the purpose of engaging in prostitution" was criminalized. That is, the Crown would have to prove that the communication involved a negotiation of a sexual service in return for payment. But the new legislation did accept two of Fraser's recommendations by clarifying the term "public place" to include the interior of a motor vehicle and by making customers as well as prostitutes liable to prosecution. The new bill became law three days after Christmas.

Street prostitutes caused most of the problems for police and commanded most of the public attention, but most prostitution— eighty percent was the common estimate—was arranged in bars and massage parlours, through dating and escort services, by a variety of modelling and photography studios, or directly through advertisements in newspapers and magazines.

During the early 1980s escort agencies in particular emerged as the most popular form of off-street prostitution. These operations flew under the radar, causing little or no nuisance to the public. When they were run carefully—that is, when operators could realistically claim that they were not responsible for what their escorts got up to— it was difficult to gather the evidence necessary to prosecute. As a result, law enforcement more or less left the escort agencies alone.

One exception to this policy of tolerance that casts light on the operations of escort services occurred in Victoria in 1985. In February, police placed wiretaps on the phones in the office of Top Hat Productions, an escort service that also offered exotic dancers and strip-o-gram delivery. As well as tapping the phones, police bugged a motel room used by the escorts and made videotapes of them having sex with clients. In May, they arrested Arlie Blakely, a forty-two-year-old grandmother who ran the operation, and charged her with nineteen prostitution-related offences. The trial, which began in November, caused a sensation because of the involvement of two Social Credit members of the Legislature, both of them cabinet ministers, as well as hints that other prominent people were implicated. One of the ministers turned out to have had nothing to do with Top Hat but the other, Industry Minister Bob McClelland, was a customer of the agency and testified at the trial. Top Hat charged customers $125 an hour for an escort, of which it retained $25. Callers placed their requests with Arlie Blakely, who then phoned escorts and told them to make arrangements with the clients. In this way the agency attempted to retain its plausible deniability, but the jury did not believe Blakely's contention that she was simply a switchboard operator. She was convicted on ten charges of living off the avails, procuring, and aiding and abetting others to engage in prostitution. She received a fine of $900 and a day in jail.[28]

The Top Hat case was an embarrassment to all concerned, not simply for Bob McClelland. Blakely's lawyer, who had been called incompetent by the trial judge, ended up being investigated by the Law Society of BC and having his right to practise suspended for six months. The Law Society didn't like the fact that he had subpoenaed one of the cabinet ministers for no reason. Meanwhile police came under a lot of criticism for videotaping sex acts and using the videos, which were not played in court, to convince witnesses to come forward. It was never clear why they had fingered Top Hat in the first place, except that it was apparently the busiest of the thirteen escort agencies in the city. If the choice was intended to deter this form of prostitution, it did not work. In any event, the case was not followed up by any campaign to shut down the agencies, in Victoria or anywhere else, for they continued to spread. By 1992 the *Vancouver Sun* reported that there were sixty escort agencies doing business in the Lower Mainland, most of them owned by only seven individuals and grossing approximately $6 million annually. There were also ten "body rub studios" that were assumed to be fronts for prostitution. The *Sun* profiled fifty-two-year-old Robert Suchy who owned nine licensed escort agencies in the city, as well as one in Whistler, and a booking agency for strippers. Suchy, who liked to stroll around town in a full-length wolf fur coat, employed about fifty women at his agencies, which had names such as Gentlemen's Fancy and Girl Next Door. His company kept close to two-thirds of the $300 fee that the women charged their customers for an hour in their company. Suchy's main competitor was Judy Boehlke, his former lover, who ran eight other agencies.[29]

Given the dangers associated with the street, and the inconvenience of being hassled by police, why didn't all women move inside? Because for all its disadvantages, the street remained the most convenient spot to meet customers and to turn the maximum number of tricks. Street encounters were usually brief: a blow job in the front seat of a car on a darkened street before returning to the stroll. For customers, the street offered affordable anonymity. By comparison, bars and clubs provided a limited number of potential clients at any one time. Also, not everyone could work for an escort agency, which required women with the requisite social skills and personalities to be "companions" as well as hookers. As Suchy explained, street prostitutes were too hardened by their experience to be good escorts. "I look for nice girls," he told the *Sun*. "Totally unexperienced. I don't hire street girls. They are too hard. Once you are out there you are spoiled."[30] Most off-street venues were not interested in women who were under eighteen years of age, or obviously doing drugs, which many street prostitutes were. According to Alexandra Highcrest, a former prostitute, many women found that working indoors was too isolated and preferred the camaraderie of the street, or at least the limited security of having someone else around to share information with about bad tricks or take down licence numbers.[31] For all these reasons, the street remained the preferred option for many sex workers.

※ ※ ※

During the early 1980s, the sexual practices of Canadians were under the microscope as never before. Not only was the Fraser Committee studying pornography and prostitution, a second federal committee was looking into a variety of sexual offences against children, including juvenile prostitution. The Badgley Committee, named for its chair, Robin Badgley, was appointed in 1981 and submitted its final report in mid-1984. Most of the public response to Badgley's report concentrated on its sensational revelations about the apparent prevalence of child sexual abuse in Canada. One-half of all female Canadians had been sexually abused, reported Badgley, and one-third of all males. These figures evoked a public outcry— from those who disputed the numbers and those who professed shock at them—that tended to obscure other parts of the report. But Badgley also revealed a disturbing prevalence of prostitution by teenagers, both male and female, under the age of eighteen. "These youth are the cast-offs of Canadian society," the report bluntly stated.[32]

The document presented a bleak picture of street youth living in a world fraught with exploitation, disease and violence, and condemned as inadequate and ineffective most previous efforts to deal with the problem.

Street prostitution is the youngest profession. Most women enter it before they are legally old enough to buy a drink, as do many boys. Youngsters work the "kiddie strolls" where customers with particular desires come to shop. The especially young, those who are under fourteen and look it, are kept by pimps in trick pads and advertised by word of mouth, on the Internet or in the want ads. The numbers of youth involved in the sex trade has always been difficult to determine, and it is misleading to lump all troubled youth in the single category of "street kids", meaning juveniles who live apart from families or foster homes and may engage in minor crime from time to time, including prostitution, in order to survive. The category contains a wide range of experiences and lifestyles. A 1979 study estimated that there were between two and three hundred teenage prostitutes working in Vancouver.[33] Ten years later, another study reported that there were three to four hundred street kids in Vancouver, though not all of them engaged in commercial sex even some of the time.[34] Nonetheless, juvenile prostitution did seem to be a growing phenomenon during the 1970s and 1980s, serious enough that Badgley devoted a great deal of his attention to it.

For Badgley, as for most people who studied the issue, the real villain in the story of juvenile prostitution was the pimp. The committee concluded that the relationship between pimp and young prostitute was one of the worst forms of abuse in Canadian society. It is "parasitic and life-destroying", the report said. "It must be stopped."[35] Pimps are young men skilled at identifying youth who are vulnerable to an approach. Recruiters hang out at movie theatres, in malls, near schools and community centres: wherever young people are in an unsupervised setting. They present themselves as friends, flatter the girls' low self-esteem, give them gifts and gradually isolate them from family, friends and social workers. Often another girl already in the life will be used to befriend the target and introduce her to the pimp. Sometimes the newcomer will be started out simply spotting for a friend (i.e., noting down car licence numbers), then be induced to start turning tricks herself. The girls develop an emotional and financial dependency on their pimps, who also exert control through physical violence and intimidation. As part of the strategy of isolation, juveniles will be moved from community to community around the western States and Canada. In the years since Badgley, different organized gangs have developed an interest in recruiting young girls for prostitution, including the Hell's Angels, the West Coast Players (a cross-border gang), and Honduran and Asian gangs.[36] Still, most pimps are not part of any large-scale criminal organization; they work independently, controlling anywhere from one to a half-dozen young women.

Convenient as it is to demonize pimps, only a percentage of youth are actively recruited into the sex trade by them. The Badgley Committee concluded that "the vast majority" of young prostitutes were not "threatened or coerced" into the business. There was no "white slave trade". At the same time, the committee recognized that pimps employed a wide range of inducements that stopped just short of coercion.[37] Like adult sex workers, many young ones described these men as boyfriends, not pimps. To the outsider, the difference might seem trifling, but to the youths, and to the law, it was crucial. Young people who sell sex are called prostitutes, but a distinction is often drawn between a youngster who occasionally may trade sex for money, food or a place to stay and a prostitute who earns a living in the business. The former activity is known as survival sex and is much more prevalent among young people than is career prostitution. The Toronto prostitute Alexandra Highcrest wrote in her memoir *At Home on the Stroll* that "there's a huge difference between seeing clients night after night because that's what you do to earn a living and turning the odd trick in order to buy some real food, or to afford a room in a decent hotel so you can get a full night's sleep."[38] As with all other sociological and economic aspects of prostitution noted over the past thirty or forty years, this continues to be the case today.

Every street kid has a unique story, but youths who get involved in the sex trade tend to share certain characteristics. Most are females in their mid-teens, though girls as young as twelve years are not uncommon. (The appearance of the AIDS virus in the mid-1980s has meant that some customers prefer to buy sex from younger teens, whom they think are less likely to be infected.) They have left home because they find their domestic situation intolerable, whether because of violence in the home, neglect, physical or sexual abuse, or some other dysfunction. Many have grown up in foster care. They are too young to have obtained job skills or training; they have trouble at school and are too angry or traumatized to make productive employees anyway. Some have underlying health problems, such as the effects of fetal alcohol syndrome. A disproportionate number are Aboriginals who have migrated to the city from their home communities and are cut off from social and family support. (A 1986 report in the *Sun*, for example, estimated that one-third of the street prostitutes in the Downtown Eastside were

Aboriginal.[39] The percentage is higher among juveniles.) They turn to sex work for the money they need to survive, but this is not healthy, safe or personally rewarding work, and so, almost inevitably, they turn to drugs and alcohol to mask their pain and fear. Which means that they need even more money, obtained in the only way they know how.

For most of these young people, getting out of the life is far more difficult than remaining in it. They have such limited employment opportunities that they cannot conceive of surviving any other way. They are alienated from the straight world; but even if they wish to leave, they have good reason to fear retaliation from a pimp/boyfriend, on whom they may have become dependent for drugs. At least the life, for all its dangers, offers a sense of community, a substitute family, that they cannot expect to find anywhere else. And perhaps the pain of street life is less than the pain of the life they left behind.

In its report, the Badgley Committee argued that juveniles engaging in commercial sex needed help, not prosecution. Social agencies should reach out to them with programmes to get them off the street and education initiatives should be used to inform youth about the risks of the lifestyle. Yet the committee did not discount entirely the use of the Criminal Code to intervene in the lives of street youth, instead making the case that in order for social agencies to do their work, an element of legal coercion had to be in place. "There is no desire on the part of the Committee to affix a criminal label to any juvenile prostitute. The Committee concluded, however, that in order to bring these children and youths into situations where they can receive guidance and assistance, it is first necessary to hold them, and the only effective means of doing this is through the criminal process."[40] Therefore the report proposed a dose of "tough love" in the form of an amendment to the Code that would criminalize the behaviour of juvenile prostitutes and allow authorities to take them into custody "in order that social intervention can take place".[41] This was one of the most controversial recommendations contained in the Badgley Report, suggesting as it did that sometimes the best way to help sexually exploited youth was to criminalize them.

Critics of Badgley argued that the report downplayed the importance of economic factors such as the lack of job opportunities to explain youth involvement in prostitution.[42] Nonetheless, the federal government responded to the report, in 1988, by passing Bill C-15 to increase protection for the victims of child sexual abuse, including sexually exploited youth. The new law made it easier to arrest pimps and increased the maximum jail sentence for living on the avails to fourteen years. It also made it illegal to solicit sex from someone under eighteen years of age. Yet little seemed to change. In subsequent years, police made few arrests under the new legislation, complaining that it was too difficult to enforce. Police decoys were ineffective, and there was little incentive for youths to alienate pimps or customers by testifying against them in court. Police were much more likely to arrest youngsters for selling sex than their customers for buying it. Even after September 1996, when the attorney general created the Provincial Prostitution Unit to deal with street youth, charges against johns were rare. A report on the subject prepared in 1997 concluded that "there is no informed understanding of the issues nor political will to protect children and youth from sexual predators..."[43]

In the middle of this debate a young street kid from Vancouver published a book that put a human face on the issue of sexually exploited youth. Evelyn Lau was fourteen years old when she left her parents' home to live on the streets. Her book *Runaway: Diary of a Street Kid* chronicles in journal form the next two years of her life. When published in 1989, the book remained on the bestseller list for thirty weeks and subsequently was made into a television movie. Unlike many runaways, Lau was not physically abused at home, but she found the situation there claustrophobic. Her parents, immigrants from China, were demanding and overprotective and would not give her the space to lead her own life. Most particularly, they did not honour her desire to be a writer. Eventually the household tensions became so great that, as an instinctive act of self-preservation, Lau left. *Runaway* gives an unremittingly bleak impression of life on the street. During her first months away from home, Lau stayed with friends and with people she barely knew. She resided in group homes, jails and psychiatric wards. She ingested a frightening amount and variety of drugs, visited her therapist regularly, bounced from social worker to social worker and thought often about suicide. *Runaway* presents a raw portrait of a teenage girl who teeters on the edge of self-destruction yet has a fierce determination to survive.

After about a year, Lau began selling sex to make money. She was fifteen. "It all began with hitchhiking", she wrote. A man gave her a ride on the Trans-Canada Highway outside of Vancouver and when he heard her story he gave her some matter-of-fact advice. "If you like your drugs and want your own place, and you want to get these things as fast as you can, then you'll have to hustle." Lau decided that she had been putting off making a decision, hoping for some better alternative. But there was no better alternative. She began "hitch hooking" that night, making $20 for giving manual sex to an elderly driver.[44] She began hanging out on Broadway near Commercial Drive. It was not one of the most popular strolls, but she had no difficulty turning tricks, primarily in cars. Much of the time she was drunk or high on drugs—Darvon, Valium, Rivotril, Mandrax, methadone, LSD. She understood the danger she repeatedly put herself in, but kept on regardless. "Believe me, prostitution is the worst sort of hell; there is no way you can convince yourself you're even human anymore." She resisted immersing herself completely in the game—"there's five black guys along Broadway who would love to be my pimp, and all I've got to do is work every night and they'd give me my apartment and all sorts of drugs."[45] Instead, she maintained her independence, working when she needed the money or when she felt herself drawn back to the life.

Lau told herself that her motives were no more complicated than the need to survive. "I'd decided to turn a trick, because I couldn't even afford a pack of cigarettes, and what could a kid do except steal, deal or trick?" But if this is true of many prostitutes, it was not true of Lau, who reveals in her book a more complicated relationship to the job. Hooking confirmed the feelings of self-loathing with which she was struggling and at the same time satisfied her desparate need to please, to be accepted, to be desired, to belong somewhere even if only on the street. For a person who was insecure and alienated and fearful of intimacy, prostitution offered a way of relating to the world that gave her a sense of control. At times Lau experienced a strong feeling of power over her customers. Yet at the same time she hated them and hated herself for going with them. And then, eventually, hooking just became something that she did. "But with prostitution, you begin to forget the motivations after a while."[46]

Eventually Lau got off drugs, got her own apartment, returned to school and left the streets. "Reality isn't easy; each day you uncover more of the illusions."[47] Remarkably, through all of this experience she held on to her literary ambitions. She continued to write and has subsequently become an award-winning poet and fiction writer. Years later she explained in an essay that far from making her more tolerant, her experiences on the street had left her revolted by the men who had abused her. "Because I knew what went on in those parked cars in the alley, the sour taste in my mouth and the sick feeling in my stomach, always the fear that something would go wrong, the vigilance for a suddenly changed mood, a flashing weapon, a curled fist. How I fled from myself through drugs and alcohol so I could be absent when those things were being done." Yet at the same time she recognized the attractions of the life. "I knew how to behave no matter what situation arose, and that was more than I could say about the other world in which I constantly struggled, trying so hard to disguise the painful shyness and awkwardness I felt. It was a way to escape, tied with the alcohol and pills that helped facilitate that escape."[48]

By the mid-1990s official attitudes towards sexually exploited youth had shifted. In 1979, when asked for her thoughts on teenage prostitution, the provincial human resources minister, Grace McCarthy, didn't think there was much her government could do. The answer to prostitution of any kind, she said, was "a better moral code within our province, within our country, and even within our world."[49] Fifteen years later, no elected or police official could be so cavalier. In the past, youth prostitution was considered a form of deliquency. Latterly it was redefined as sexual victimization, a form of child abuse. The attention of law enforcement shifted to the customer. Police began to view youths not as criminals but as victims and to divert them to social agencies instead of the courts. Police and social workers developed strategies for preventing youth involvement in sex work, limiting the dangers that it involved and getting young people off the street and back into school, jobs and satisfactory living situations. Yet the issue of sexually exploited youth remained a difficult one. Interviewed in 1989, one outreach worker said, "One has to remember that these kids are self-destructive; they're victims, they're unaware of legal processes, they're unaware of the consequences of health risks—social diseases, and AIDS; they're unaware of the risk of being beaten up and raped [...] What they're doing is really impulsive and self destructive; they're in crisis."[50]

Street prostitution is much like a bubble of mercury. When you press down on it in one place, it slithers away and pops up somewhere else. The 1984 injunction banning prostitutes from the city's West End had its predictable result. The women and youths simply relocated, in this case east of Granville to a stroll along Seymour and Richards streets and also into the Mount Pleasant neighbourhood near Broadway and Main. The former became the most densely populated stroll, accommodating up to half of the street prostitutes in the city, but because the district was mainly commercial, their presence was tolerated. Most strolls expand in area as they become known and more women arrive to take advantage of the heavy traffic. Not so the Seymour/Richards stroll, where one police officer reported that "the prostitutes seem to be willing to stand 15 abreast and keep it confined basically to a two block area."[51] Once the new communicating law was in place at the beginning of 1986, police used undercover officers, both male and female, posing as hookers or johns, to gather evidence. In the case of the Seymour/Richards stroll, however, police hardly ever used female decoys because there were so many working women on the street that the decoy would get lost in the crowd and not make enough contacts to produce a worthwhile sting. As John Lowman pointed out in his 1989 assessment of the new law, this meant that johns who frequented the downtown stroll, who tended to be wealthier because prices were higher, were largely immune from prosection, whereas in Mount Pleasant, where decoys were used extensively, most customers were working stiffs. As a result, Lowman concluded, most of the men prosecuted under the new law came from "the lower end of the socio-economic scale."[52]

Prostitution in Mount Pleasant was more contentious than downtown because the women drifted into the residential side streets and the people who lived there were not happy to see their neighbourhood becoming the "new West End". By November 1984 the *Sun* was reporting that between thirty and sixty women were working in the neighbourhood.[53] Some local people took a conciliatory attitude towards them. The local residents' association struck a committee that came out against the vigilantism and heavy-handed court actions that had influenced events in the West End. Instead it recommended working with the prostitutes to come up with solutions to problems such as traffic congestion, noise and drug dealing. As time passed, however, residents lost patience with the hookers and began pressuring the city to get them out of the area. Some wondered why Attorney General Brian Smith did not ask the courts to issue an injunction, as he had done in the case of the West End, but Smith was reluctant to use such a drastic measure again. In fall 1985, city council approved $30,000 to improve street lighting in the warehouse district to the north of what had become the Mount Pleasant stroll, hoping to encourage the women to take their business there. Much was made of this supposed red light district in the press, but for a variety of reasons the idea did not work out. Because the location was more isolated, the women felt less safe there; local businesses objected; and police continued to arrest prostitutes who did move, violating an agreement that the women thought they had with the authorities. Meanwhile, at the end of the year, the new federal legislation came into effect and police warned that they would be stepping up their efforts to clear the prostitutes out of Mount Pleasant. In 1986, police formed a special task force intended to discourage street activity. During the summer months this force flooded the area with patrols, setting up roadblocks, ticketing drivers for minor traffic infractions and hanging around working women to frighten off potential customers. And it worked. After two summers police were reporting less prostitution in Mount Pleasant.

Displaced from Mount Pleasant, some prostitutes migrated back to the Downtown Eastside where, beginning in 1986, they spread along Hastings east of Main and into the residential streets of Strathcona. Prostitutes had been working in this part of the city since early in the twentieth century, but in the past they had kept mainly to the commercial areas. Strathcona residents were alarmed to see an influx of working women on their sidewalks and in their parks, and the usual antagonisms ensued. In consultation with the community, however, street workers came up with a novel way of avoiding confrontations. In 1987 they distributed a map indicating parts of the neighbourhood that prostitutes should consider no-go areas: streets close to schools, daycare facilities, playgrounds and parks. "We are asking you, as fellow parents and members of the community, to avoid certain areas where families live, and children play and go to school", read a note that accompanied the map. "Please keep your business to non-residential areas."[54] Police could not endorse the map formally, but they did focus their activities on people who were working within the no-go zones, and by and large the prostitutes, at least the experienced, older ones, honoured the community's wishes. One street worker explained that "historically in the Downtown East Side there have always been areas where it has been OK for women to work – there was a large measure of social acceptance of prostitution. I think people down here understood that women were out there as a result of economic circumstances, so there wasn't the same sort of labelling and name calling that went on in Mount Pleasant."[55] Generally speaking, police did a better job of mediating between prostitutes and residents in Strathcona than in others parts of the city and as a result the level of conflict was kept to a minimum.[56]

In 1989 the federal government commissioned a series of studies to evaluate the impact of Bill C-49, the "communicating" law. John Lowman, the SFU criminologist who had carried out a similar study for the justice department in 1984, was asked to prepare a report for Vancouver. The new law was enforced mainly by undercover cops posing as participants in the trade. Lowman described the strange dance that occurred as a prostitute tried to discover whether the john she was approaching was an actual customer or a decoy. For the purposes of the law, the fake customer had to manipulate the prostitute into mentioning a sex act and an asking price, while the prostitute endeavoured to conclude a deal without being explicit by using a variety of code words, numbers or hand signals. Many prostitutes asked to touch the prospective client's crotch or asked the client to expose himself or touch their breasts, believing, usually correctly, that police would not do so. Despite this ludicrous cat-and-mouse game at which prostitutes were becoming increasingly adept, police reported that they had little difficulty satisfying the requirements to make an arrest. After interviewing prostitutes, social workers, police and attorneys, Lowman concluded that Bill C-49 was doing nothing to decrease the incidence of street prostitution in the city. He criticized the new law for addressing the concerns of residents and other anti-prostitution lobbyists without answering the fundamental question: If not here, where? Where were prostitutes supposed to work? As long as this question was ignored, street prostitutes were simply shunted from neighbourhood to neighbourhood. Lowman rejected the argument that stiffer sentences would have an impact. He compared the law to "a badly repaired car". The answer was not to tinker with it. The answer was to junk it and get a new one, or better yet, to find a new way of getting around altogether.[57]

As awareness of the inadequacies of the law grew, the matter was submitted in 1990 to the Supreme Court of Canada for its opinion. Asked about the constitutionality of the law, the Court ruled that the communicating law was indeed a violation of Section 2(b) of the Canadian Charter of Rights, the section guaranteeing freedom of expression to every Canadian. The justices ruled that the law, by criminalizing a private conversation between two people, violated that right. But the majority of the justices also found that under Section 1 of the Charter, it was reasonable to limit freedom of expression in this case in order to control the various forms of nuisance that arose from the public sale of sex. The Court was also asked to rule on a Section 7 challenge to the communicating law. Section 7 of the Charter guarantees that "everyone has the right to life, liberty and security of the person and the right not to be deprived thereof except in accordance with the principles of fundamental justice." Opponents of the communicating law argued that it made the conditions under which prostitutes worked more dangerous, thereby infringing on their right to life and security. Because they were unable to carry on their profession, which was, after all, legal, without fear of arrest and possible incarceration, prostitutes also faced an infringement of their right to liberty. Three of the justices, including the two women on the court, agreed with these arguments, though the majority did not and the law was allowed to stand. With this weak endorsement by the Supreme Court, the federal government felt itself under no immediate pressure to change the law. As ineffective, even dangerous, as the communicating law appeared to be, for the time being the status quo would prevail.

Five

THE MISSING WOMEN

On the night of 14 September 1996, Michael Leopold, a thirty-four-year-old labourer, set out to conduct an experiment. He drove to the Downtown Eastside where he picked up a street prostitute and took her to a nearby parking lot. As the woman began to give him oral sex, he punched her in the head and tried to jam a rubber ball into her mouth to keep her quiet. His plan was to abduct, torture, rape and eventually murder her. Instead, the woman put up a fight. Her screams brought help and Leopold fled into the night, leaving behind his pager and a length of knotted rope. Three days later, police arrested him and charged him with assault. While in custody Leopold revealed to a psychiatrist named Roy O'Shaughnessy that the incident in the parking lot was a trial run. If it had been successful, he intended to act out his sadistic fantasies by brutalizing and killing more prostitutes. He had made a torture chamber in the basement of his house where, he said, he planned to disfigure the bodies so that they could not be identified before he disposed of them in the bush. O'Shaughnessy had been hired by Leopold's lawyer, so their conversations ordinarily would have been protected by lawyer-client privilege. But O'Shaughnessy petitioned the Supreme

Court of Canada to make an exception and in 1999 the court ruled that the psychiatrist could testify at trial about what he had heard. The judge who presided over Leopold's case, describing him as a "sexual sadist" and a high risk to reoffend, sentenced him to fourteen years in prison.

Leopold was a sexual predator who targeted prostitutes because they were isolated and vulnerable. Prostitutes have always provided easy prey for killers. Jack the Ripper, who murdered five streetwalkers in the Whitechapel district of London in 1888, is the most infamous but he was certainly not the first. More recently the South Side Slayer in Los Angeles tortured and murdered fourteen women, mainly African-American prostitutes, between 1983 and 1987. And in 2003, the Green River Killer was convicted of strangling forty-eight women, most of them prostitutes, in Washington State. The tragic irony of all the attempts by police and lawmakers to herd street prostitutes into non-residential neighbourhoods and to scare off their customers was that such actions left the women increasingly vulnerable to men like these: merciless, twisted killers who preferred to hunt their prey in the shadows. And there are a lot of them. In 2001, police drawing up a list of possible suspects in cases involving attacks on and murders of sex workers in British Columbia ended up with the names of six hundred men in the community who were known to prey on women.[1]

In May 1995, a study prepared for a coalition of groups in the Downtown Eastside revealed that 99 percent of sex workers had been assaulted on the job, often several times a year. This number included 62 percent who said that they had been sexually assaulted, 52 percent who were beaten by a boyfriend, 48 percent who were beaten by a customer, 31 percent who were attacked with a knife and 30 percent who were assaulted with some other weapon. They had been strangled, dragged by cars, beaten with fists, robbed, raped and pistol whipped.[2] Strange to say, Michael Leopold's victim was one of the lucky ones. She survived. Many did not.

During the 1990s, articles began appearing in the newspapers about a chilling surge in the number of prostitutes being murdered in Vancouver. Before 1975, no sex workers were known to have been murdered in the city. Then, slowly, inexorably, the number began to climb. Three murders in the late 1970s; eight murders between 1980 and 1984; twenty-two during the remainder of the decade. The bodies of these women were discarded in construction sites, vacant lots, ditches, dumpsters, and hotel rooms where they lived and worked. Few of the perpetrators were ever caught. The toll continued to rise until by September 2001 the number over two decades had reached more than sixty, an average of three a year. Over half of the cases remained unsolved.[3]

Most of the murdered women came from the Downtown Eastside. Women from the "high track" Richards Street stroll were not the ones being killed, nor were call girls working for escort agencies or masseurs working in body-rub parlours. It was street prostitutes working the "low track" around Hastings and Main and farther east. As one woman told the journalist Daniel Wood, catching tricks on the Downtown Eastside had become like a game of Russian roulette. "How many shots do I have left? How long until I get to the chamber that's not empty?"[4] Always a poor neighbourhood, neglected and looked down on by the rest of the city, the Downtown Eastside during the 1980s and 1990s was ravaged by addiction and the spread of HIV/AIDS. About 16,000 people make their home there, attracted by the cheap housing, the drugs, the action. About forty percent of the population is Aboriginal. The rest are a polyglot mix from all over the world, plus, of course, a dwindling number of original residents: elderly, retired men who once knew the place as Skid Road and now subsist on disability pensions and social assistance. According to Statistics Canada, the neighbourhood has the lowest per capita income in Canada. Young kids who have left their family homes or foster care to experiment with life on the streets are attracted by the activity, danger and access to drugs. In 2000, there were an estimated 4,700 injection drug users in the Downtown Eastside, probably the highest concentration of any city in the country.[5] Heroin, crack cocaine and a variety of uppers and downers are freely available on the streets. The use of injection drugs has led to soaring rates of hepatitis C and HIV infection. Death by drug overdose is common. In 1997 the city declared a public health emergency when it was discovered that HIV infection rates were the worst in the developed world. Since the government decided during the 1970s to empty the mental institutions, the area had also become home to an estimated five hundred mentally ill people, some homeless, others not. Some were women engaged in sex work to survive. In the Downtown Eastside, all the pain and dysfunction of modern urban life were on display, unprotected by wealth or privilege. What's more, the area was seen by the rest of the city as a moral wasteland, a plague spot, a dumping ground for the socially disabled, a haven for criminals and drug addicts who made the district a dangerous place to venture into. Isolated from the rest of the city by contempt and fear, it was the perfect setting for anyone looking to prey on the weak and vulnerable.

What accounts for the rise in violence against street sex workers? Prostitution always has been a risky business, but never so risky as it has become. There have always been violent men taking advantage of women who work the streets, but never with such frequency as now. It is impossible to believe that the cause is anything other than misguided public policy. Almost everyone agrees in hindsight that it was a mistake to flush women out of the nightclubs where they had established a reasonably safe work environment. The increase in the incidence of prostitute murders begins in 1975, the same year as the infamous police raid on the Penthouse. But this was just the beginning of a series of events and policies that put the lives of street sex workers at risk as they had never been before.

As more women, and young men, took to the streets, neighbourhood groups, police and local politicians responded by forcing them into increasingly more isolated and dangerous parts of the city. In the late eighties, fewer hotels rented rooms by the hour for the women to use because they were afraid of being charged as brothels. This left women to conduct their business in cars, alleyways and deserted parking lots. Generally speaking, sex workers in the Downtown Eastside were more likely to be addicted to drugs and alcohol, and addicted women took less care to evaluate their dates for potential trouble. Another factor was the 1986 communicating law. Many prostitutes complained that it made their work more dangerous. Predators knew that women who were assaulted were unlikely to complain to police; they were, after all, breaking the new law. Now that any talk about sex for money was illegal, negotiations had to be conducted quickly and often inside the motor vehicle, forcing women to make split-second decisions about whether it was safe to go with a customer.

To avoid police, prostitutes turned tricks in dark out-of-the-way places. "A lot of girls go with their dates down to beach areas and wooded areas in order to keep away from the police," said one woman, "and it's dangerous because they don't know if the john will bring you back. There is nobody there to keep an eye out for you."[6] The courts began imposing area restrictions as a term of probation. Women convicted of prostitution-related offences were excluded from the stroll where they had been working, which simply meant that they relocated either to the edge of the stroll, thus expanding it, or to a new neighbourhood altogether. Banned from particular areas, some began hitch-hooking alone, a dangerous alternative to the company of the stroll. Stereotypically, street women have pimps who are supposed to watch out for them, and some do. In reality, though, pimps who are concerned about the safety of their women are rare. Most prefer to keep a low profile so as to avoid the police. In all these ways, women were forced by the law, and by law enforcement, to engage in practices that increased their vulnerability.

As the murder count rose, the enormity of the situation sank in only slowly. In March 1992, the *Sun* ran a five-part series on the sex trade called "Dollars and Sex". The series led off with a curious article that seemed to suggest that the most serious problem with the sex trade was that the government was losing revenue by not taxing it. The series focused on the operations of escort agencies and other indoor venues, not the street. One article mentioned the unsolved murders of prostitutes, but did not point out that the murder rate was escalating or suggest that there was any urgency about protecting the women.

During the mid-1990s, the issue of prostitution in residential neighbourhoods heated up again. Police decided to focus on the customers and in August 1994 mailed "Dear John" letters to thirty-four men whose cars were seen trolling for prostitutes in Mount Pleasant and Cedar Cottage to the southeast. The letters asked the men to stay away from the areas and reminded them that many hookers were juveniles.[7] Meanwhile, residents of Mount Pleasant and the Wall Street area mounted shame-the-johns campaigns to encourage customers to leave their neighbourhoods. In Strathcona the previous summer, posters had appeared on telephone poles warning prostitutes to "move out or face the consequences".[8] Fearing a repetition of the uproar in the West End, the federal justice minister, Allan Rock, announced that he was contemplating stiff new penalties to get hookers off the streets, including impounding cars belonging to johns, allowing police to fingerprint and photograph johns and prostitutes (even though neither had necessarily broken the law) and raising prison sentences for pimping to five years. "Street prostitution has laid waste to a whole area of cities", said Rock. "Property values have diminished markedly, people can't raise their kids safely, there are needles in the street, used condoms in the schoolyard. The whole trade is accompanied with a raft of unpleasant aspects that are completely unacceptable." Mayor Philip Owen was elated at the thought of these measures being implemented, but in the end, none of them was.[9] More importantly, despite the unprecedented violence being inflicted on the women, the discourse surrounding street prostitution still focused on nuisance factors in the neighbourhoods. Even though women were dying, there was no mention of policies that might protect them from the men who were preying on them.

On 25 June 1997, Janet Henry disappeared from the Downtown Eastside. A thirty-six-year-old Aboriginal woman from Alert Bay, she had been working as a prostitute for several years to support a drug habit acquired following the breakup of her marriage. She knew the desperation of the streets. She had been raped by at least one customer and had had a gun held to her head by another. She was last seen in the beverage room of the Holborn Hotel.

Henry used to telephone her sister, Sandra Gagnon, every day, so when she stopped calling, Gagnon started looking. She filed a missing persons report, put up posters and scoured the downtown. There was a lot of evidence that Henry had not simply decided to leave town—she did not take her personal belongings or the money in her bank account, and she had just recently paid up her next month's rent—but no evidence of her whereabouts. Neither her sister nor her daughter have heard from her since.

Janet Henry is one of the sixty-eight human beings who have become known as the Missing Women. She was not the first to disappear, but she seems to have been the first whose disappearance was noticed beyond a circle of friends or family. When she could find no sign of her sister, Sandra Gagnon talked to a newspaper reporter, Lindsay Kines, who wrote a story for the *Sun* a month after Henry's disappearance, thus setting in motion a chain of events that forced police to acknowledge that dozens of women had gone missing from the Downtown Eastside over the years. Most were sex workers, many of them struggling with addiction. Eventually the investigation led police to a farm in the suburb of Port Coquitlam and what may turn out to be the most deadly serial killer in Canadian history.

A year after Janet Henry's disappearance, Vancouver police acknowledged for the first time publicly that they were concerned at the number of women who seemed to have gone missing from the Downtown Eastside. The number then stood at sixteen, and police had decided to review the cases in search of links. The spectre of a serial killer was raised, though at this point police said they had no indication that the women had been targeted, or even murdered. Yet the issue was beginning to tug at the edge of the public's consciousness. "I don't think the public really understands the degree of risk that children and women on the street selling themselves are experiencing these days", the social worker John Turvey told the *Sun*. "It is phenomenally dangerous out there." The headline on the story read "Serial killer not behind missing-women cases, police official says".[10] It was the first use of the phrase "missing women". The phrase stuck. The case of the Missing Women was born.

One of the women whose disappearance had attracted the attention of investigators was Sarah de Vries, a twenty-eight-year-old prostitute and mother. In this case, unlike most of the others, there was a precise record of the vanishing. Early on the morning of 14 April 1998, after spending the previous evening with a friend, she left her room at the Beacon Hotel and began working the corner of Princess and Hastings. Another woman who was working across the street got picked up for a date that didn't work out and returned to the corner a few minutes later. In the time it took to drive around the block, Sarah had disappeared.

Sarah de Vries also had a sister. Maggie de Vries is a writer, teacher and book editor, and when one of Sarah's friends told her that he had not heard from Sarah in a week, she immediately reported her missing. Maggie, who later wrote a moving book about her sister called *Missing Sarah*, talked with police, plastered the Downtown Eastside with posters showing Sarah's photograph, gave interviews to reporters and pleaded for tips from the public. But it did no good to know when and where her sister had been abducted, what she was wearing, the fact that she wrote poetry and had two children. There were still no witnesses, no evidence, no sign of her at all.

At first, police were reluctant to admit that the cases of Sarah de Vries, Janet Henry and the others were linked, or that anything bad had happened to the women. These are individuals in a mobile profession with marginal ties to the community, they said. Maybe they just left town. Finding everyone who chooses to get lost is not a police officer's job. These arguments betrayed a lack of understanding of the personal lives of those involved. As Maggie pointed out, sex workers are not transients.[11] Despite their unconventional lifestyles, many of the women had routines. They picked up their welfare cheques; they phoned family and friends; because many were sick with AIDS or hepatitis, they had medical appointments; they had children; they had personal effects that they would have taken with them. There was plenty of evidence to indicate they had been snatched.

When pressed to explain their apparent lack of progress, police pointed out that they had a hard time investigating such cases. Often a great deal of time had passed between when a woman was last seen and when she was reported missing. If a woman had no family or friends with whom she was in regular contact, weeks, even months, might go by before the disappearance was noted. The longer the time lag, the more difficult it was for police to construct a sequence of events and find witnesses who might remember seeing something. Victim and perpetrator were strangers to each other. Their lives intersected only in a moment of violence. Nothing linked them but the crime. There were too many suspects, the hundreds of men known to be capable of harming prostitutes. There was no crime scene. And of course, there were no bodies and none of the forensic evidence that bodies provide. In Canada generally, approximately eighty percent of all murders are solved and convictions are obtained. When it comes to the murders of street prostitutes, the success rate falls to about a quarter.[12]

As family and friends complained that police were not taking the disappearances seriously enough, the department announced in September 1998 that it had created a working group to investigate the cases of forty Vancouver women who had gone missing since 1971, sixteen of whom had disappeared from the Downtown Eastside in the previous three years. "We're in no way saying there is a serial murderer out there," insisted a police spokesperson. "We're in no way saying that all these people are dead. We're not saying any of that." What they did appear to be saying was that some sort of a pattern was emerging to suggest that at least some of the missing women were part of the same case. As Maggie de Vries put it, "it starts to seem more and more as if there's something happening. There's a pattern to this."[13]

Now that the disappearances had been noticed, police began receiving tips from the public. Among these calls was an anonymous one received in fall 1998 about a pig farm in Port Coquitlam. The call was investigated, but neither the Vancouver police nor the RCMP were able to get enough information at that time to justify a search warrant for the property. Meanwhile, women continued to disappear.

By early March 1999, the tally of women unaccounted for during the past four years had reached twenty. Family members and advocates for the women insisted that they must have been the victims of foul play, but police continued to say that they had no evidence that this was the case. "These women have completely disappeared from the face of the Earth", one advocate said. "If they are not murdered, where are they?"[14] At about this time someone raised the idea of offering a reward, a tactic resisted by the police and initially by Mayor Philip Owen as well. The notion seemed to focus the frustration some people were feeling about the lack of progress in the case and the lack of respect being given to the Missing Women. Its supporters hoped it would result in some useful tips, but police argued that such an offer would just stimulate a flood of information that they had no way of verifying because they had no witnesses or hard information to go on and might actually put the life of a missing woman in jeopardy. As yet there was no officially acknowledged crime, so how could there be a reward? But in April, Mayor Owen changed his mind and announced that the city and the province would put up $100,000 for information about any foul play involving the Missing Women. For the first time, years after the first of the women had disappeared, a public official was acknowledging publicly that the women may have been crime victims.

On 12 May, Sarah de Vries's thirtieth birthday, more than four hundred people crowded into the pews at First United Church at Hastings and Gore in the heart of the low-track stroll to attend a memorial for her and the other missing women. The church was decorated with tulips and everyone wore a burgundy ribbon. As each woman's name was read, friends or relations came forward to light a candle. The service lasted two and a half hours, so that everyone who wanted to had time to share their feelings. Afterwards, those present each took a tulip and joined a march that wound its way through the streets to the waterfront and Crab Park, where a plaque was unveiled in memory of the missing. The plaque is still there, on a bench looking out over the harbour.

Following the memorial service, events temporarily picked up momentum. In July the popular television crime show *America's Most Wanted* aired a segment on the missing women. Ujjal Dosanjh, the provincial attorney general, appeared at a press conference with John Walsh, the host of the programme, to release a poster displaying photographs of the thirty-one women whom police were trying to track down. The poster specified that the $100,000 reward was "for information leading to the arrest and conviction of the person or persons responsible for the unlawful confinement, kidnapping or murder" of any of the women. At about the same time, the police department created a special Missing Women's Review Team to work the investigation. (Subsequently this team would be revealed to have been woefully understaffed and inexperienced.[15]) DNA was collected from the families of the Missing Women to allow bodies to be identified, if and when any were found. In November, the Toronto magazine *Elm Street* published an article about the disappearances by Daniel Wood, bringing the case to the attention of a national audience for the first time. Wood raised the possibility that there was a serial killer or killers targeting low-track prostitutes. He was unflattering in his portrayal of Mayor Owen and the police whom he suggested had been indifferent to the fate of the women for too long.

Publicity did not bring results, however, and women continued to disappear, six during 1999, another two towards the end of 2000, eight more during 2001. In spring 2001, the police investigation was transferred from the Vancouver department to a joint team of ten RCMP and city officers created to review the cases yet again. Members of the joint forces team were not long on the job before they came up with an additional fourteen disappearances that seemed to fit the profile, bringing the number to forty-five.[16] These new figures were revealed in the first of a series of articles on the disappearances that ran in the *Sun* during the fall. The articles were critical of the way police had handled the investigation, citing the frustration of family members and documenting a variety of shortcomings including inadequate staffing, infighting among members of the review team, computer problems and the mishandling of suspects. Partly as a result of the articles, police began meeting with families of the Missing Women to keep them informed, and the review team was reconstituted as a full-fledged Missing Women Joint Task Force of sixteen officers.

On the morning of 1 December 2001, the news carried a chilling story for anyone who cared about the fate of Vancouver's Missing Women. Police in Washington State announced that after almost twenty years they had made an arrest in the Green River murders. Gary Ridgway was a non-descript, fifty-two-year-old truck painter. Initially he was charged with the murder of four women; in time the number of murder charges climbed to forty-eight. Almost all his victims were young prostitutes who worked along a commercial strip of the Pacific Highway near the Sea-Tac Airport south of Seattle. Two young boys had discovered the first body floating in the Green River in summer 1982. Subsequently bodies were found in the river and at various dump sites around King County. For a while, the Green River Killer was the most notorious active serial killer in North America. But after 1985 he seemed to go to ground and public interest waned. The police continued their pursuit, however, and as it became clear that a serial killer was preying on Vancouver prostitutes it was theorized that the Green River Killer might have been active north of the border. Vancouver police consulted with their Washington State colleagues, but no link was ever found. In December 2003, Ridgway was convicted of the murders and sentenced to forty-eight life terms in prison without possibility of parole.[17]

Meanwhile, in Vancouver, police were actively investigating their own mysterious disappearances, pressured by the disgruntled families and an impatient media, but there was no particular reason to think that a break was going to take place soon. After all, the investigation had dragged on for several years without tangible results. Then, on Thursday, 7 February 2002, the task force called a press conference to announce that officers were beginning to search a farm on Dominion Avenue not far from the Pitt River in Port Coquitlam. Earlier in the week they had visited the property on the pretext of looking for firearms and had discovered evidence linked to at least two of the missing women. The second warrant inaugurated the most thorough and macabre search in BC criminal history. It lasted almost two years. The farm, and another property nearby, were cordoned off behind a wire fence. Dozens of officers in white coveralls scoured the site. Heavy earth-moving equipment was used to sift through dirt and debris looking for human remains and other clues. The entire site was divided up into grids and the soil from each one searched for evidence. In June, a team of fifty-two archaeology students from universities across Canada joined the hunt, examining the dirt and debris as it passed by on conveyor belts, looking for bone fragments. (They were joined by another fifty-one students the following spring.) Two forensic anthropologists were also involved. The implications of such a meticulous and grisly search for the fate of the Missing Women was left to the public's imagination. The investigation was "forcing light onto a part of our society that traditionally resides in the very dark shadows", said RCMP Constable Cate Galliford at one of the media briefings.

> Most people in society don't give a second thought about what's really happening on the streets of our cities. And some people don't want to think about it. This investigation is uncovering very new territory for many in the public [...] and the news media. The way most people understand something new is by comparing it to past experiences and existing knowledge. But the world this investigation is publicly exposing [...] is nothing like most people have even dreamed about...."[18]

The search involved two properties, the farm on Dominion Avenue and a second lot nearby on Burns Road, both owned by three members of a family named Pickton. The farm was 6.8 hectares in size, scattered with buildings, mounds of landfill and debris, and old cars. It was flanked by a golf course and suburban housing built on land that previously had been part of the Pickton property until the family sold it. It became known in the press as the "pig farm", though neighbours told reporters that while the Picktons still bought and sold the animals, they no longer raised them. A building on the Burns Road site attracted special attention from investigators. It was a warehouse-sized structure known as Piggy's Palace where wild parties and pig roasts were reported to have been held.

Two weeks after the search began, police arrested one of the owners of the property, Robert William Pickton, fifty-two, known as Willy, and charged him with two counts of first-degree murder. The two victims were identified as Mona Wilson and Sereena Abotsway, both from the Downtown Eastside. Wilson was twenty-six years old when she disappeared in November 2001, a veteran of the low-track stroll where, according to her boyfriend, she turned tricks to support an addiction to heroin. Abotsway had disappeared in August 2001 shortly before her thirtieth birthday. She had entered foster care when she was four years old, already the victim of sexual abuse. As a teenager she moved to a group home where the other kids, more streetwise than she was, introduced her to the downtown life. Her former foster mother said Sereena suffered from fetal alcohol syndrome.

"We believe we now have answers regarding the disappearance of two missing women", said Constable Galliford. "But this is a case involving 50 missing women. There are a lot of questions still unanswered."[19] One of those questions, of course, was why it took so long for police to move on the farm. Pickton had been a suspect in the case since the earliest tip came in to police in July 1998; and more than a year earlier, in March 1997, he had been charged with attacking a prostitute with a knife, but the charges were stayed. For some reason police did not fully pursue the tips they received for four years. The media were quick to point out that during this time, thirty more women had gone missing, some of whom Pickton eventually would be charged with killing.

As the search continued at Pickton's property and the evidence piled up, so did the charges against him. On 2 April, he was charged with three more murders; a week later, a sixth; on 22 May, a seventh; four more on 19 September; and another four on 2 October. Each time Willy Pickton appeared in court to face the new charges, the public got another glimpse of him in the news: his feral-looking face with its sharp features, scraggly beard, high forehead and long disheveled hair. Rumours swirled through the city about what had actually gone on at the farm and why an arrest had not been made sooner. Repeated calls were heard for a public inquiry into how police had handled the Missing Women investigation.

In November 2003, the Missing Women Joint Task Force announced that their search of the Port Coquitlam properties was complete and that they were pulling out. Every inch of the properties had been scoured for evidence, every building taken apart. Whatever the site could reveal about the fate of any of the Missing Women had been revealed. Work continued with the analysis of evidence gathered at the site, and in May 2005 Willy Pickton was charged with twelve more murders, bringing the total to twenty-seven. If convicted, he will become the most prolific serial killer in Canadian history. Among the latest group of identified victims was Sarah de Vries. The Pickton trial began early in 2006, by which time police had identified sixty-eight women as missing, with disappearances dating back to 1978. More than half of them are Aboriginal. The trial of Pickton, whatever its outcome, will not answer all the questions about the fate of most of these women. That some of the Missing Women have fallen victim to a sexual predator or predators seems highly likely. In 1999, the *Sun* reported that its records showed that during the previous seventeen years at least twenty-five different men had been charged with killing prostitutes in BC.[20] In a way, a single serial killer would be a relief. Then police could set their sights on catching him and ending the slaughter of street women.

But it is not that simple. There are hundreds of men known to be capable of vicious sex crimes, and doubtless hundreds more who have given no cause for suspicion. As Maggie de Vries wrote in her book about her sister, "we err if we believe that the problem stops with whatever occurred on a single farm in Port Coquitlam."[21] To take just one example: in December 2003, Vancouver police arrested a forty-year-old hotel worker named Donald Michel Bakker in Crab Park after being alerted by the screams of a sex worker. They found videotapes in Bakker's possession showing other sex workers being assaulted. A search of his home produced further tapes showing more sadistic assaults, as well as sexual acts with young girls over-seas. One officer called them the most disturbing images he had seen in his twenty-five-year career. Bakker, who was married with a young child of his own, had never before come to police attention. Apparently he hired women to engage in sadistic sex, then hurt them far more than they had agreed.[22] He was charged with twenty-two counts of assault against local prostitutes as well as more charges relating to the foreign incidents, but eventually pleaded guilty to ten counts and was jailed for ten years.

In a paper that he published in 2000, the Simon Fraser University criminologist John Lowman argued that "several" serial killers prob-ably were involved in the slayings of sex workers in British Columbia over the past twenty years. But he also thought that the serial killer scenario did not fully explain what was happening. Instead, he identified a "systematic pattern of violence against pros-titutes perpetrated by many men, some of whom are serial killers." In other words, many serial killers murder prostitutes, but not all prostitute murderers are serial killers. They are violent males who are encouraged by society's attitude to sex workers and abetted by laws that force the women into the shadows where no one is looking. Sometimes these predators are "practising" on prostitutes, whom they know are vulnerable, and will move on to other women as their confidence grows. Lowman went on to say that "violence against prostitutes ought to be understood as part of a continuum of violence against women more generally".[23] Gary Ridgway, the convicted Green River Killer in Washington State, told the judge at his trial that he chose to murder prostitutes from the highway strip where he trolled for victims because "they were easy to pick up without being noticed. I knew that they would not be reported missing right away, and might never be reported missing. I picked prostitutes because I thought I could kill as many of them as I wanted without being caught."[24] No one could say it any more clearly. Predators target sex workers because they think that they can get away with it, and they think they can get away with it because our laws and our attitudes make it possible for them to do so.

Six

SEX AND THE CITY

In the city of Vancouver, sex is for sale almost everywhere. After 120 years of crusading politicians, police crackdowns and moral panics, there are more prostitutes at work than at any other time in the city's history. Most of these sex workers, male and female, never put in a professional appearance on the street. They work from home or at one or another of the indoor venues where sex is transacted. Some of these places—massage parlours, steambaths, modelling agencies, "health enhancement centres", acupressure clinics, small residential brothels—are visited by clients. Others, such as dating services and escort agencies, provide sex to go. Many such venues hold valid business licences from the city. In 2006, the cost of a licence to operate a body rub parlour was $8,158; for an escort service, $1,008; for a dating service, $178. Some of the services offered are exactly as advertised, but many are not and everyone knows it. Technically they are breaking Canada's prostitution laws. But unless they do something to bring themselves to the attention of authorities, these businesses operate with impunity. So also do the hundreds of women and men who advertise for customers in the want ads of local newspapers such as the *Georgia Straight* and *Xtra West*. Far and away the largest category in the classified advertisement section of the weekly *Straight*, for example, is "adult services", which includes phone sex, female masseuses, escorts of every nationality, male and female, dominatrixes and transgendered "she-males". Every fetish and sexual practice is accommodated.

The Internet has been for the off-street sex worker what the telephone was for the call girl—a way of making direct contact with customers away from the prying eyes of police and public. The Internet is used also to share information about places where sex is for sale. Browsers in the virtual world can view advertisements for massage parlours such as the Swedish Touch ("relaxation and entertainment spa for men") and escort agencies such as After Midnight, and view provocative photographs of hundreds of women and men who are offering their companionship directly to the client. Chat rooms and message boards allow satisfied customers to recommend where the "best" services can be found. Anyone with a rudimentary knowledge of computers can now set up shop in the sex trade. The stereotype of the streetwalker in mesh stockings loitering against a lamppost and leaning into car windows has given way to the image of the young career girl or guy making dates on a BlackBerry. In time, surely this new world of prostitution will provide the setting for a television sitcom.

It has been estimated that about eighty percent of Vancouver's commercial sex is transacted indoors. That leaves twenty percent, somewhere between two and three hundred women and men, selling sex on the streets each night. These outdoor sex workers are concentrated in three main areas. The high-track stroll is located around Helmcken and Richards streets where it has been more or less since the courts evicted prostitutes from the West End in the mid-1980s. The high-track stroll is controlled by pimps, and customers pay top dollar. Drugs are not prevalent here because the pimps do not want their women addicted. Yet drug use on the street is almost inevitable, and those women who suffer the effects of addiction may slide inexorably towards the medium track, located along Kingsway. This is a larger area where some women manage to work independently while others are controlled by pimps. The low track is the Downtown Eastside where many of the women and girls are survival sex-trade workers, working the street to support an addiction, willing to turn tricks for as little as the price of the next fix. The only pimps on the low track are boyfriends or husbands, often addicts themselves, whom the women support. About one hundred male prostitutes, two dozen transgendered ones and thirty to forty youth share the streets with these women every night. In total, then, there are at least two thousand people—men, women, teenage boys and girls—engaging in the sex trade in the city on a day-to-day basis, and many believe that figure to be conservative.

※ ※ ※

In his book *The Natashas: The New Global Sex Trade*, the investigative journalist Victor Malarek describes a stretch of highway just inside the Czech Republic near its border with Germany. For five kilometres, Highway E-55, the main road between Dresden and Prague, is lined with prostitutes, women from Ukraine, Romania, Russia and other Eastern European countries who are forced into sexual slavery by pimps who have purchased them from traffickers. The women may have been lured into the trade by promises of employment, bought from orphanages or forcibly abducted. Under the eye of the pimps, they stand at the side of the road attracting the attention of male motorists who have driven to this outdoor super-market to buy sex. Transactions are conducted in the fields and wooded areas nearby. Many of the women are drug addicted or infected with sexually transmitted diseases, or both. When they become pregnant, their babies are put out for adoption.[1] Their plight is eerily evocative of the women who haunt the streets of Vancouver's Downtown Eastside.

The women along Highway E-55 are part of a worldwide traffic in Eastern-bloc women that has boomed since the disintegration of the Soviet Union in 1989. Malarek estimates that every year 175,000 women are recruited in the former Soviet republics and trafficked to pimps in the West who put them to work as prostitutes, usually against their will or in conditions they never contemplated. The women, who are told they must work to repay their "debts", are engaging in an illegal activity in a foreign country where they often do not even speak the language. Their choices are limited. And Eastern Europe is just one source of trafficked women. According to Malarek, it represents a "fourth wave" of a global sex trade that ear-lier concentrated on bringing women from Asia, Africa and Latin America to fill the brothels and sex parlours of Western Europe and North America.[2]

The international sex traffic has roots in Vancouver. Young women were brought here from China and Japan to work as prosti-tutes from early in the twentieth century. Organized trafficking on a larger scale, however, began to come to the attention of police in the early 1990s. In the fall of 1991, immigration officials at the Vancouver International Airport turned back twenty-one teenage Malaysian girls who they said were being brought into the country by organized gangs to work as prostitutes. A week later, six Korean men were arrested in the city and charged with running "an international prostitution ring". The head of the police vice squad, Don Keith, explained that Asian gangs, Korean and otherwise, were flying in women and girls from Malaysia, Indonesia and the Philippines. The girls were not told what would be expected of them in Canada, said Keith, and they were kept more or less as slaves by the pimps who were in charge of them.[3] Periodic police raids confirmed that the traffic continued in the Vancouver area and that it was organized and sometimes gang related. Early in 1998, for example, five Malaysian women were discovered working in a brothel in Richmond that police claimed was connected to a local Asian gang, the Big Circle Boys.

Another offshoot of the international sex trade has been the spread of so-called microbrothels throughout suburban neighbourhoods. These are small operations of just a few women run out of private homes or apartments. Many of the women are foreign nationals brought to the city solely to work in the brothels. An investigation by the *Vancouver Sun* in 2004 claimed that two hundred of these neighbourhood operations were active in the Lower Mainland. It was not clear whether the women may have been sex workers in their native countries who knew they were coming to Canada to ply their trade or whether they were being held as prisoners. As usual, police complained that it was too time consuming for them to gather the evidence necessary to shut down the microbrothels, which therefore operated more or less freely.[4]

Concern about the international sex traffic is reminiscent of the white slavery panic that gripped Europe and North America at the turn of the twentieth century. One hundred years ago the fear was that innocent young white women were being abducted and forced into sexual slavery by dark-skinned "foreigners". Today it is the women who are the foreigners, stolen from their homes in Asia and Eastern Europe and put to work against their will in brothels and strip clubs in the West. The modern sex traffic seems to be well documented, though it is worth remembering that the white slave trade was as well, and it turned out to exist more in the fevered imaginations of middle-class moralists than in reality. In the same way that the white slave panic mobilized public opinion in support of laws against prostitution a hundred years ago, the modern global traffic is sometimes used to argue for the suppression of prostitution. In *The Natashas*, for instance, Victor Malarek contends that legalizing prostitution in western countries leads inevitably to a massive influx of trafficked women controlled by organized crime.[5] According to this argument, the amelioration of laws against prostitution at home results in the sexual exploitation of unfortunate women from abroad. Yet there are laws against illegal immigration, violence against women, forcible confinement and other aspects of people trafficking, and it is difficult to see why they are not sufficient to deal with the issue of imported sex workers without invoking stronger laws against prostitution. In fact, it is sometimes argued that the situation of foreign sex workers would be much improved if sex work in Canada generally were decriminalized, regulated or both. At any rate, as far as Vancouver goes, the global sex traffic so far plays a small role.

❋ ❋ ❋

As a political issue in Vancouver, street prostitution is the elephant in the room: no politician wants to talk about it seriously. During the civic election campaign in November 2005, when one candidate suggested that the city should open its own brothel and endorsed the creation of a red-light district, the others backed away from the issue as though it were radioactive. Following the election, Mayor Sam Sullivan (who, during the campaign, said he was not running for mayor to be a pimp and called the proposals for a red-light district or a publicly-owned brothel "crazy") confessed that while he wanted to "improve life" for street sex workers, he had no concrete plan to do so.[6] This in a city that as far as the sex trade is concerned is the murder capital of North America. Mayor Sullivan drew a distinction between "a short-term problem you fix" and "a long-term problem you manage", suggesting that street prostitution is the latter. In fact it is both. Obviously prostitution has been around for a long time and authorities have always found ways of "managing" it so as to limit its nuisance side effects. But prostitution is also a short-term crisis. Women have been dying in the city in unprecedented numbers, and there is evidence that the law is at least partly at fault.

Policing is a dangerous profession. Since 1886 and the creation of the Vancouver Police Department, sixteen officers have died on the job. But compare that to the 107 cases of murder in which the victim was a sex-trade worker, all of them in the past few decades. Other professions are more deadly. To take one prominent example, forty-three forest workers died on the job in British Columbia in 2005 alone. But there is no other line of work in which people face the extraordinary level of assault and murder as they do in sex work. Some say that the women choose to do what they are doing. Aside from whether choice is the right word, police officers and loggers also choose their work, knowing it is dangerous, yet no one suggests that it is acceptable that their lives be imperilled.

Sex workers themselves feel that their lives are devalued by the rest of society. A report written for PACE, the Vancouver prostitutes' advocacy group, argued that "no amount of rhetoric can disguise the fact that the lack of any substantive response by all three levels of government can be traced to the simple fact that since it is only street level sex workers that are being raped and murdered it does not, and most likely will not, matter."[7] Whether this cynical attitude is justified, there does seem to be a growing consensus that while society does not need to be protected from prostitutes, prostitutes need to be protected from society, or at least its more violent members. At the same time, there is no consensus about how this might be accomplished. At one end of the scale of opinion, abolitionists believe, as they have for more than a century, that the best thing for society, and for sex workers themselves, is to eradicate prostitution by imposing new laws and enforcing old ones. At the other end, decriminalizers advocate removing prostitution from the Criminal Code altogether. Decriminalizers would allow prostitutes to function as any other small-business person with a service to sell, leaving them to be regulated and licensed in the same ways. Somewhere between these two poles are the legalizers who would like to see prostitution become legal in certain controlled circumstances: for instance, in government-regulated brothels or supervised red light districts.

Even given modern permissive attitudes towards sex, abolition continues to enjoy strong support, mainly from religious moralists and some elements of the women's movement. The argument of the abolitionists is a simple one: prostitution exploits women and therefore should not be tolerated. Abolitionism is based on two assumptions:

that commercial sex is bad (otherwise, why abolish it?) and that bad things should be legislated out of existence. Most abolitionists admit that no level of law enforcement will eradicate all prostitution. But, they argue, just because the law is not one hundred percent effective is no reason to get rid of the law. We don't think this way about murder, and we shouldn't think this way about prostitution. To an abolitionist, when authorities turn a blind eye to the sex industry, they are approving an activity that at the least enslaves and degrades women and at the worst puts their lives in peril. The idea that government at any level would license and/or operate a brothel or legislate a red light district puts the state in the position of acting as a pimp. It also legitimizes prostitution as a career choice for young women, leading to an increase in the ranks. Abolitionists have even argued that, in a legalized situation, jobless women could be required to work as prostitutes instead of receiving unemployment benefits.[8]

Most abolitionists think that prostitutes are little better than slaves, forced into the business by poverty, sexual abuse and coercive pimps. They want public policy to do something about these fundamental causative factors as a way of eradicating prostitution. They want the authorities to enforce, or even stiffen, the laws against prostitution, while at the same time providing alternatives for women who want to leave the business and return to the mainstream of society. Many abolitionists are feminists who believe that legalisation would not address the harm that prostitution does to the women and young men who are its victims. While they believe that prostitutes should not be prosecuted, they advocate increasing penalties against customers, pimps and anyone else who profits from the trade. This is the so-called "Swedish model", based on the example of Sweden where it is illegal to buy sex or to live off its avails but not to sell it.

Advocates for the legalization or the decriminalization of sex work argue that abolition flies in the face of experience and the facts. First of all, they say, it is impractical to think that laws against prostitution are enforceable. A much larger police force would be needed to devote full time to shutting down all the escort agencies, massage parlours, microbrothels, call girls and Internet sites doing business in the city. Even modest attempts to eliminate street prostitution in Vancouver have failed, and failed miserably, serving only to redistribute the activity and put the women at risk. Campaigns aimed at discouraging customers, they argue, have had little success for the same reason. The men will go elsewhere and the women will follow. As one sex worker told an interviewer: "For every girl that gets arrested and taken off the street, there is another girl to replace her. For every trick that gets arrested, there is another one to replace him. It just goes in circles."[9]

Secondly, sex workers do not think of themselves as victims. "Sex work exists now, has always existed and always will exist," Maggie de Vries argues in her book *Missing Sarah*.

And many sex workers, including those who work on the street, do not do drugs. Some find sex work provides them with a better income to support their families than any other work available to them. Even those involved in survival sex do have some freedom to choose and cannot be forced to change their lives. While they may be having sex for money because it is their only means of survival, of keeping a roof over their head, of getting food and feeding their drug habit, they are not slaves.[10]

Some women may feel that selling themselves is the only economic opportunity available to them; some street kids may be driven by desperate circumstances to engage in commercial sex. But these are the minority. Few people working in the wide variety of venues for commercial sex are being coerced. The job pays better than a lot of others and it may be more convenient than other work, or offer more personal independence. Hard as it may be for some people to accept, there are many reasons why a sex worker might choose his or her profession, and not all of them have to do with victimization.

Abolitionists demonize pimps, and justifiably so. Pimps account for much of the violence against street sex workers and the threat they pose to youngsters whom they wish to entice into prostitution is real. Those in favour of decriminalization, however, argue that the way the present law is written criminalizes anyone living off the earnings of a prostitute, including a husband, a lover, a friend, perhaps even a child. Pretty much anyone having a relationship with a prostitute can be prosecuted. As Alexandra Highcrest pointed out in her memoir, one finds violent, exploitive men living off the earnings of women in all kinds of professions. Why single out prostitutes?[11] There are laws protecting women against violence and abuse. Why are these not adequate to the job of protecting sex workers from violent pimps?

For the most part, legalizers and decriminalizers think that there is no reason for the law to interfere in a private arrangement between consenting adults. They agree that there is a role for the law in controlling the nastier side issues: the public nuisances, the coercion, the violence, the involvement of youth. Where they diverge is on the question of whether existing laws can do this. Decriminalizers seem to believe that they can, or should be amended so that they will. Legalizers believe there is still a role for the state in regulating commercial sex so as to ensure that sex workers are not exploited and other members of society not inconvenienced. They would legalize prostitution, but within limits, say in licensed brothels or on safe strolls. These measures are a recognition of the same harm-reduction principle that was behind the creation of the safe injection site for intravenous drug users on the Downtown Eastside in 2003. Sex work is going to go on; it is the responsibility of the public to discover ways it can go on with the least harm to its participants. Since the city already licenses escort agencies, massage parlours and other businesses that are sometimes fronts for prostitution, legalizers wonder why it would balk at endorsing similar settings that might help street-based sex workers.

Some level of unregulated street prostitution would continue even if brothels and safe strolls were legalized. A regulated sex trade would not welcome underage youths, or sex workers who were sick or for whatever reason did not accept a regulated system. Just as some women still work the street today, even though they can work indoors as escorts or masseuses, so others would continue to be independent operators even if legalized venues were available. The hope of legalizers is simply that a regulated sex trade would be better than the dangerous, hypocritical situation that exists today.

Anyone who has studied prostitution acknowledges that it is only partly a legal issue. No law, or set of laws, is ever going to make prostitution disappear, or make sex workers completely safe from male violence. No law is going to solve the problems of poverty, abuse, homelessness and addiction that lead many women and young people to enter the trade. No law is suddenly going to improve the lives of young urban Aboriginals. Sex workers need laws, but they also need choices. In other words, they need policies that do something about the social and health problems that lead disadvantaged women and youth to think that prostitution is the only choice they have.

✳ ✳ ✳

That said, laws can make things worse, and the prostitution laws almost surely do. First of all, they are confusing. To paraphrase Stan Persky, if prostitution is legal, which it is, and free speech is legal, which it is, how can it be illegal to speak freely about prostitution? Yet it is.[12] The PACE report summed up the bizarre state of the law as it relates to commercial sex. "It's legal to sell sex in Canada but if you sell it on the street you can be arrested. If you sell it in your home you can be arrested. If you open a business to sell it, you can be arrested. If you help somebody sell it you can be arrested."[13]

Secondly, the laws are capricious, or at least the enforcement of them is. Police appreciate having laws on the books that allow them to charge prostitutes, johns and pimps whenever they wish. Even when they recognize that arresting a sex worker is merely revictimizing her, police argue that they need some form of legal coercion to encourage women to quit the trade. Police also appreciate being able to charge johns, some of whom they argue may be potentially dangerous sexual predators, and pimps, some of whom prey on young children. But laws are not made for the convenience of police, they are made for the protection of the public. The only people who need protecting are the sex workers themselves. The law apparently does exactly the opposite by putting them in jeopardy. Present laws are also discriminatory because they are aimed at street prostitutes, who are mainly poor, addicted, Aboriginal women and youths, while being ineffective against the much larger off-street trade. Eighty percent of prostitution in Vancouver takes place off the street, yet the street trade accounts for ninety-five percent of prostitution-related criminal convictions.[14]

Lastly, the current laws may well be unconstitutional. Although the Supreme Court of Canada ruled in 1990 that provisions of the Criminal Code dealing with prostitution were constitutional, circumstances have changed; some legal opinion holds that if the Court were asked to render another decision, the outcome would be different. In a report prepared in 2005, the Pivot Legal Society, a group of legal activists in Vancouver, argued that the increased level of violence experienced by sex workers during the past two decades represents a violation of their fundamental rights to life, liberty, security, equality and free speech, as guaranteed by the Charter of Rights and Freedoms, and that the nuisances associated with commercial sex are far less important than the harm being done to the women who engage in it.[15]

Early in 2005, Ottawa decided to take yet another look at the laws surrounding prostitution. Almost everyone seemed to agree that the current ones were inadequate. Awareness that predators were victimizing street prostitutes as never before added a new urgency to the debate. So in March a subcommittee of the House of Commons justice committee set out to cross Canada to investigate what was actually taking place on the streets of the largest cities. As they toured the country, the five MPs heard from police, prostitutes, academics and anyone else who came forward with an opinion about the issue. By the end of the year they were reportedly ready to issue a report advocating some form of legalization, when the minority government in Ottawa fell. The subcommittee disbanded, and the country plunged into a winter election. The result of the campaign was another minority government, this time led by Stephen Harper and his Conservatives. Given its socially conservative views, it seems doubtful that a Harper government will do anything to ease the laws against prostitution, though in the middle of 2006 the parliamentary subcommittee was reconstituted and began preparing its report. Law reform, for the time being at least, appears to be a dead issue.

Most of us no longer think of prostitutes as pariahs. But the image of the modern prostitute remains unclear. Is she, and now he as well, a victim of a) sexual abuse, b) the patriarchy, c) male depravity, or d) the law? Is she or he a criminal corrupter from whom the rest of us need to be protected, or a skilled professional who simply needs better working conditions to perform a socially productive job? The short answer is yes. Prostitutes are all of the above, at least in stereotype, and because we cannot agree on what prostitution is, we cannot agree on what we should do about it. History reveals a surprising consistency to the debate. Police always have wanted laws on the books that allow them to keep prostitution within tolerable limits and within certain neighbourhoods. Moralists have rejected this approach, preferring instead an all-out war on prostitution, which they believe corrupts society and debases women. Politicians have either avoided the issue as too hot to handle or exploited it to win votes. The majority of the public have usually been willing to ignore it so long as it wasn't going on in their neighbourhood.

Meanwhile, most prostitutes have managed to find a position for themselves that will allow them to carry on their work without attracting the attention of the law, though the illegal nature of their work leaves them without the rights afforded other workers. The

minority of prostitutes who work the streets have been less fortu-
nate. They continue to work in conditions that for any other profession would be considered intolerable. If anything good could
possibly derive from the case of the Missing Women, perhaps it will
be that this terrible episode, which has forced the issue of prostitution to the forefront of the public agenda, has made it impossible to
ignore any longer the contradictions in our laws and in our attitudes.
Change must come. One dares to hope that after 120 years, the
time has arrived to give sex workers the same tolerance and protection as every other resident of the city.

Notes

INTRODUCTION

1. Daniel Francis, *L.D.: Mayor Louis Taylor and the Rise of Vancouver* (Vancouver: Arsenal Pulp Press, 2004).

2. Daphne Marlatt and Carole Itter, eds., *Opening Doors: Vancouver's East End* (Victoria: Province of British Columbia, Sound Heritage Series, vol. XIII, nos 1–2, 1979), pp. 61–62.

ONE: Women at Work, 1873–1914

1. Joe Swan, *A Century of Service: The Vancouver Police, 1886–1986* (Vancouver: Vancouver Police Historical Society, 1986), p. 13.

2. City of Vancouver Archives (hereafter CVA), Fire Insurance Plan of Granville Townsite, August 1885, map 334.

3. J.S. Matthews, *Early Vancouver*, Vol. 1 (Vancouver: Brock Webber Printing, 1932), pp. 135–37.

4. Jean Barman, *The Remarkable Adventures of Portuguese Joe Silvey* (Madeira Park, BC: Harbour Publishing, 2004), pp. 25–27.

5. Robert A.J. McDonald, *Making Vancouver, 1863–1913* (Vancouver: UBC Press, 1996), p. 59.

6. Matthews, *op.cit.*, pp. 150–51.

7. M. Allerdale Grainger, *Woodsmen of the West* (Toronto: McClelland and Stewart, 1964), pp. 14–15; originally published in 1908.

8. Robert A. Campbell, *Demon Rum or Easy Money: Government Control of Liquor in BC from Prohibition to Privatization* (Ottawa: Carleton University Press, 1991), p. 18.

9. Constance B. Backhouse, "Nineteenth-Century Canadian Prostitution Law: Reflection of a Discriminatory Society", *Social History*, vol. XVIII, no. 36 (Nov. 1985), p. 395.

10. Betty Keller, *On the Shady Side: Vancouver 1886–1914* (Ganges, BC: Horsdal & Schubart, 1986), p. 81.

11. Ethel Wilson, *The Innocent Traveller* (Toronto: McClelland and Stewart, 1949).

12. Swan, *op.cit.*, p. 20.

13. CVA, Police Department Records, Series 202, Prisoners' Record Books 1898–1902, loc. 37-C-8, pp. 66–67.

14. *Daily Province*, 18 and 25 August 1903.

15. *Ibid.*, 3, 7 and 21 March 1904.

16. *Ibid.*, 23 April 1904.

17. CVA, Police Department Records, Series 202, Prisoners' Record Books 1898–1902, loc. 37-C-8.

18. *Daily Province*, 2, 15 and 26 June 1906.

19. Keller, *op.cit.*, p. 46.

20. *Daily Province*, 8 August and 3 Nov. 1906.

21. Timothy Gilfoyle, *City of Eros: New York City, Prostitution, and the Commercialization of Sex, 1790–1920* (New York: W.W. Norton and Co., 1992), p. 203.

22. *Daily Province*, 3 Nov. 1906.

23. *Ibid.*, 17 June 1907.

24. Deborah Nilsen, "The 'Social Evil': Prostitution in Vancouver, 1900–1920", *In Her Own Right: Selected Essays on Women's History in British Columbia*, Barbara Latham and Cathy Kess, eds. (Victoria: Camosun College, 1980), p. 224, n. 31.

25. *Daily Province*, 24 Dec. 1906 and 16 March 1907.

26. *Ibid.*, 19 Nov. 1906.

27. Nilsen, *op.cit.*, p. 213.

28. Daniel Francis, *L.D.: Mayor Louis Taylor and the Rise of Vancouver* (Vancouver: Arsenal Pulp Press, 2004), pp. 93–94.

29. Alan Artibise, *Winnipeg: A Social History of Urban Growth, 1874–1914* (Montreal: McGill-Queen's University Press, 1975), pp. 254–55.

30. James H. Gray, *Red Lights on the Prairies* (Toronto: Macmillan of Canada, 1971), p. 50.

31. *Globe*, 12 Nov. 1910.

32. For a full description of these events, see Gray, pp. 44–57; Artibise, pp. 253–64; and Rhonda L. Hinther, "The Oldest Profession in Winnipeg: The Culture of Prostitution in the Point Douglas Segregated District, 1909–1912", *Manitoba History*, no. 41 (Spring/Summer 2001), pp. 2–13.

33. John McLaren, "White Slavers: The Reform of Canada's Prostitution Laws and Patterns of Enforcement, 1900–1920", *Criminal Justice History*, vol. 8 (1987), p. 54.

34. *Daily Province*, 28 March 1912.

35. *Social Vice in Vancouver*, report issued by the Moral and Social Reform Council of BC, June 1912.

36. *B.C. Federationist*, 22 June 1912.

37. *Daily Province*, 3 Dec. 1912.

38. *Daily Province*, 26 Nov. 1912.

39. *Sun*, 2 Dec. 1912.

40. *The Truth*, 28 Nov. 1912; Joe Swan, *op. cit.*, p. 32.

41. Linda Eversole, *Stella: Unrepentant Madam* (Victoria: Touchwood Editions, 2005).

42. Gilfoyle, *op. cit.*, pp. 163ff., 241.

43. McLaren, "White Slavers", pp. 90–94.

44. CVA, Board of Police Commissioners, Series 180, Minutes, 5 Jan. 1915, p. 151.

TWO: The Social Evil Between the Wars

1. The official transcript of the Lennie inquiry is at CVA, Vancouver Police Department Records, Series 209, 11 volumes, 37-D-6, 37-D-7, 37-D-8.

2. CVA, Vancouver Police Board, Series 181, 75-C-1, file 1, Report of R.S. Lennie, Commissioner, Vancouver Police Inquiry, 1928, pp. 10–21.

3. *Ibid.*, p. 25.

4. *Daily Province*, 11 Oct. 1928.

5. CVA, Mayor's Correspondence, Series 483, 33-B-5, file 1, Report to Mayor by the legal advisor to Col. Foster, 16 Feb. 1935, p. 6.

6. Ivan Ackery, *Fifty Years on Theatre Row* (Vancouver: Hancock House, 1980), p. 108.

7. *Sun*, 10 Dec. 1934.

8. Vincent Moore, *Angelo Branca: Gladiator of the Courts* (Vancouver: Douglas & McIntyre, 1981), p. 181.

9. David Ricardo Williams, *Mayor Gerry: The Remarkable Gerald Grattan McGeer* (Vancouver: Douglas & McIntyre, 1986), p. 172.

10. *Daily Province*, 12 April 1935.

11. *Ibid.*, 2 April 1935.

12. *Sun*, 5 March 1958.

13. Ian Macdonald and Betty O'Keefe, *The Mulligan Affair* (Surrey, BC: Heritage House, 1997), p. 125.

14. Marlatt and Itter, *Opening Doors*, p. 144.

15. For a history of this neighbourhood, see John Atkin, *Strathcona: Vancouver's First Neighbourhood* (Vancouver: Whitecap Books, 1994).

16. Jo-Ann Canning-Dew and Laurel Kimbley, *Hastings and Main: Stories from an Inner City Neighbourhood* (Vancouver: New Star Books, 1987), p. 72.

17. *Opening Doors*, p. 32.

18. *Ibid.*, p. 81.

19. *Ibid.*, p. 52.

20. *Ibid.*, p. 156.

21. A. Katsuyoshi Morita, *Powell Street Monogatari* (Burnaby, BC: Live Canada Publishing, 1988), p. 65–67.

22. Marlatt and Itter, *Opening Doors*, p. 104.

23. Wayde Compton, *Bluesprint: Black British Columbian Literature and Orature* (Vancouver: Arsenal Pulp Press, 2001), p. 19.

24. *Opening Doors*, p. 51.

25. *Ibid.*, p. 141.

26. Lennie Inquiry transcript, *op. cit.*, p. 50.

27. *Ibid.*, p. 565.

28. *Ibid.*, p. 127ff.

29. *Ibid.*, p. 50.

30. *Ibid.*, p. 192ff.

31. Patricia Roy, *Vancouver: An Illustrated History* (Toronto: James Lorimer & Co., 1980), p. 99.

32. Ackery, *Fifty Years*, p. 107.

33. Greg Marquis, "Vancouver Vice: The Police and the Negotiation of Morality, 1904–1935", in Hamar Foster and John McLaren, eds., *Essays in the History of Canadian Law. Vol. VI: BC and the Yukon* (Toronto: University of Toronto Press, 1995), p. 260.

34. Williams, *Mayor Gerry*, p. 205.

35. Swan, *A Century of Service*, p. 62.

36. CVA, Mayor's Correspondence, file 1-3, Report of Chief Foster to the Police Commission, 18 Jan. 1935.

37. *Ibid.*, Memo re. Certain Vice Conditions in the City of Vancouver, Sept. 5, 1935.

38. Roy, *Vancouver*, p. 123.

39. *Sun*, March 22, 1920; *Daily World*, 16 Jan. 1922.

40. Kay J. Anderson, *Vancouver's Chinatown* (Montreal: McGill-Queen's University Press, 1991), p. 113.

41. See Hilda Glynn-Ward, *The Writing on the Wall* (Toronto: University of Toronto Press, 1974 ed.).

42. Emily Murphy, *The Black Candle* (Toronto: Thomas Allen, 1922), pp. 169, 188.

43. Tom McInnes, *Oriental Occupation of British Columbia* (Vancouver: Sun Publishing, 1927), p. 53.

44. Patricia Roy, *The Oriental Question: Consolidating a White Man's Province, 191–41* (Vancouver: UBC Press, 2003), pp. 43–44.

45. Paul Yee, *Saltwater City* (Vancouver: Douglas & McIntyre, 1988), p. 98.

46. Denise Chong, *The Concubine's Children* (Toronto: Penguin Canada, 1994), p. 83.

47. *Vancouver Sun*, 16 Sept. 1937.

48. For a discussion of this episode, see Kay Anderson, pp. 158–64.

49. *Globe*, 7 June 1917.

50. Jay Cassel, *The Secret Plague: Venereal Disease in Canada, 1838–1939* (Toronto: University of Toronto Press, 1987), p. 163.

51. Marquis, *"Vancouver Vice"*, p. 258.

52. Cassel, *Secret Plague*, p. 216.

53. Robert A. Campbell, *Sit Down and Drink Your Beer: Regulating Vancouver's Beer Parlours, 1925–54* (Toronto: University of Toronto Press, 2001), p. 24.

54. *Ibid.*, p. 90.

55. Donald H. Williams, "The Suppression of Commercialized Prostitution in the City of Vancouver", *Journal of Social Hygiene*, vol. 27, no. 7 (Oct. 1941), p. 365.

56. *Ibid.*, p. 372.

57. See Michaela Freund, *The Politics of Naming: Constructing Prostitutes and Regulating Women in Vancouver, 1934–1945*, MA thesis, Simon Fraser University, 1995, pp. 46–58.

58. Marlatt and Itter, *Opening Doors*, p. 32.

THREE: From Brothels to Bars: Prostitution in the Postwar City

1. Williams, *Mayor Gerry*, p. 276.

2. See Macdonald and O'Keefe, *The Mulligan Affair*.

3. Personal interview, 10 Nov. 2005.

4. *Sun*, 12 January 1959.

5. *Ibid.*, 11 Nov. 1960.

6. For example, *Sun*, 24 Oct. 1958.

7. *Province*, 8–13 Nov. 1952.

8. Peter Trower, *Dead Man's Ticket* (Maderia Park, BC: Harbour Publishing, 1996), p. 27.

9. Personal interview, 18 May 2006.

10. Canning-Dew and Kimbley, *Hastings and Main*, pp. 152–54.

11. *Sun*, 28 June, 4 Oct. 1966.

12. Andersen, *Vancouver's Chinatown*, p. 186.

13. Canning-Dew and Kimbley, *Hastings and Main*, p. 157.

14. John Lowman, "Submission to the Subcommittee on Solicitation Laws of the Standing Committee on Justice, Human Rights, Public Safety and Emergency Preparedness", 2005, p. 3.

15. Deborah Brock, *Making Work, Making Trouble: Prostitution as a Social Problem* (Toronto: University of Toronto Press, 1998), p. 22.

16. Royal Commission on the Status of Women, *Report* (Ottawa: Information Canada, 1970), p. 370.

17. *Ibid.*, p. 372.

18. Monique Layton, "Prostitution in Vancouver (1973–1975): Official and Unofficial Reports", Report submitted to the BC Police Commission, Sept. 1975, p. 103.

19. G.A. Forbes, "Street Prostitution in Vancouver's West End", Report prepared for Vancouver Police Board and Vancouver City Council, 7 Sept. 1977, p. 10.

20. *Sun,* 8 July 1976.

21. Layton, "Prostitution", p. 147.

22. Harkema, personal interview.

23. *Sun,* 8 July 1976.

24. Robert M. Welsh, *Sex, Vice and Morality: Tales from a Detective's Notebook* (Vancouver: self-published, 1994), p. 112.

25. *Ibid.*, p. 123.

26. Layton, pp. 172–73.

27. *Ibid.*, p. 110.

28. *Ibid.*, p. 53.

29. Forbes, "Street Prostitution", p. 6.

30. Layton, "Prostitution", p. 111.

31. Forbes, "Street Prostitution", p. 2.

32. John Mackie and Sarah Reeder, *Vancouver: The Unknown City* (Vancouver: Arsenal Pulp Press, 2003), p. 179.

33. *Globe*, 20 April 1978.

34. Layton, "Prostitution", p. 104ff.

35. *Sun*, 22 Dec. 1977.

36. Harkema, personal interview.

37. *Sun*, 22 Feb. 1977.

38. *Ibid.*, 3 Dec. 1976.

39. John Lowman, "Vancouver Field Study of Prostitution", *Working Papers on Pornography and Prostitution, Report No. 8*, vol. 1 (Ottawa: Dept. of Justice, 1984), p. 278.

40. *Sun*, 3 and 22 Oct. 1983; 1, 7 and 14 June 1984; 3 Oct. 2002.

FOUR: There Ought To Be a Law

1. John Lowman, "Street Prostitution" in Vincent F. Sacco, ed., *Deviance: Conformity and Control in Canadian Society* (Scarborough, Ont.: Prentice-Hall Canada, 1992), p. 72.

2. John Lowman, "Prostitution in Vancouver: Some Notes on the Genesis of a Social Problem", *Canadian Journal of Criminology*, vol. 28, no. 1 (Jan. 1986), p. 11; Stan Persky, *The House That Jack Built: Mayor Jack Volrich and Vancouver Politics* (Vancouver: New Star Books, 1980), p. 62ff.

3. *Globe and Mail*, 15 April 1978; Nick Larsen, "The Politics of Prostitution Control: Interest Group Politics in Four Canadian Cities", *International Journal of Urban and Regional Research*, vol. 16, no. 2 (June 1992), p. 174; *Province*, 29 March 1981.

4. Larsen, "Politics of Prostitution Control", p. 173.

5. *Province,* 13 August 1977.

6. *Sun*, 9 May 1980.

7. *Province*, 10 Sept. 1977; 7 August 1980.

8. *Sun*, 30 Oct. 1979.

9. Robert Wilson, *The Wendy King Story* (Vancouver: Langen Communications, 1980).

10. *Ibid.*, p. 112.

11. *Sun*, 19 Dec. 1980.

12. *Sun*, 9 Dec. 1983; 13 and 16 Jan. 1984.

13. See Lowman, "Vancouver Field Study".

14. *Ibid.*, p. 191.

15. *Ibid.*, p. 194.

16. *Ibid.*, pp. 231, 234.

17. Special Committee on Pornography and Prostitution. *Pornography and Prostitution in Canada*, (Ottawa: Dept. of Supply and Services, 1985), vol. 2, p. 346; *Sun*, 12 Jan. 1984.

18. *Sun*, 20 Feb. 1982.

19. *Sun*, 7 April 1982.

20. *Sun*, 10 May 1982.

21. *Sun*, 3 March 1983.

22. *Province*, 24 June 1983.

23. *Province*, 29 June 1984.

24. Special Committee on Pornography and Prostitution, *Pornography and Prostitution in Canada*, vol. 2, p. 394.

25. *Ibid.*, pp. 417ff., 425.

26. *Ibid.*, pp. 534, 547, 551.

27. John Lowman, Vancouver Field Study, p. 366.

28. *Sun*, 28 Sept., 4 Oct., 20 Nov., 17 Dec. 1985.

29. *Sun*, 20–21 March 1992.

30. *Sun,* 20 March 1992.

31. Alexandra Highcrest, *At Home on the Stroll* (Toronto: Knopf Canada, 1997), p. 44.

32. Committee on Sexual Offences Against Children and Youths, *Sexual*

Offences Against Children (Ottawa: Ministry of Supply and Services, 1984), vol. 1, p. 91.

33. *Sun*, 7 July 1979.

34. John Lowman, *Street Prostitution: Assessing the Impact of the Law, Vancouver* (Ottawa: Dept. of Justice, 1989), p. 139.

35. *Sexual Offences,* vol. 2, p. 1061.

36. Renata Aebi, "The Trafficking in Children for the Purpose of Prostitution: British Columbia, Canada", Paper prepared for the National Judicial Institute, International Instruments and Domestic Law Conference, Montreal, 9–12 Nov. 2001, p. 5.

37. *Sexual Offences*, vol. 2, p. 992.

38. Highcrest, *At Home*, p. 131.

39. *Sun*, 12 April 1986.

40. *Sexual Offences*, vol. 1, p. 95.

41. *Ibid.*, vol. 2, p. 1046.

42. See, for example, Brock, *Making Work*, p. 132.

43. Kimberly Daum, *A Cast of Contradictions* (Vancouver: Downtown Eastside Youth Activities Society, Sept. 1997), pp. 1, 3.

44. Evelyn Lau, *Runaway: Diary of a Street Kid* (Toronto: HarperCollins, 1989), p. 161ff.

45. *Ibid.*, pp. 173, 185.

46. *Ibid.*, pp. 166, 203.

47. *Ibid.*, p. 181.

48. Evelyn Lau, "The Shadow of Prostitution", *Inside Out: Reflections on a Life So Far* (Toronto: Doubleday Canada, 2001), pp. 14–15.

49. *Sun*, 7 July 1979.

50. Quoted in Lowman, *Street Prostitution: Assessing the Impact of the Law*, p. 171.

51. *Ibid.*, p. 102.

52. *Ibid.*, p. 63.

53. *Sun*, 13 Nov. 1984.

54. Lowman, *Street Prostitution*, p. A-434.

55. *Ibid.*, p. 176.

56. Nick Larsen, "The Politics of Law Reform: Prostitution Policy in Canada, 1985–1995" in Larsen and Burtch, eds., *Law in Society: Canadian Readings* (Toronto: Harcourt Brace & Co., 1999), p. 64.

57. Lowman, *Street Prostitution*, p. 210.

FIVE: The Missing Women

1. *Sun*, 23 Nov. 2001.

2. Sue Currie, *Assessing the Violence Against Street-Involved Women in the Downtown Eastside/Strathcona Community* (Vancouver: Downtown Eastside Youth Activities Society, 1995); *Sun*, 17 May 1995.

3. *Sun*, 21 Sept. 2001.

4. Daniel Wood, "Missing", *Elm Street* (November 1999).

5. Leonard Cler-Cunningham and Christine Christensen, *Violence Against Women in Vancouver's Street Level Sex Trade and the Police Response* (Vancouver: PACE Society, 2001), p. 18.

6. Pivot Legal Society, *Voices for Dignity: A Call to End the Harms Caused by Canada's Sex Trade Laws* (Vancouver, 2005), p. 16.

7. *Sun*, 9 August 1994.

8. John Lowman, "Violence and the Outlaw Status of (Street) Prostitution in Canada", *Violence Against Women*, vol. 6, no. 9 (Sept. 2000), p. 1004.

9. *Sun*, 22 Sept. 1994.

10. *Sun*, 3 July 1998.

11. Maggie de Vries, *Missing Sarah: A Vancouver Woman Remembers Her Vanished Sister* (Toronto: Penguin Canada, 2003), p. 189.

12. Lowman, "Violence and the Outlaw Status", p. 992.

13. *Sun*, 18 Sept. 1998.

14. *Sun*, 3 March 1999.

15. *Sun*, 22 Sept. 2001.

16. *Sun*, 21 Sept. 2001.

17. The Green River case is documented in Ann Rule, *Green River, Running Red* (New York: Free Press, 2004).

18. RCMP news release, 20 March 2002.

19. *Ibid.*, 22 Feb. 2002.

20. *Sun*, 3 March 1999.

21. De Vries, *Missing Sarah*, p. 220.

22. *Sun*, 17 Jan. 2004.

23. Lowman, "Violence and the Outlaw Status", pp. 999, 1008.

24. Rule, *Green River*, p. 618.

SIX : Sex and the City

1. Victor Malarek, *The Natashas* (Toronto: Viking Canada, 2003), pp. 24–28.

2. *Ibid.*, p. 6.

3. *Province*, 11 and 15 Sept. 1991.

4. *Sun*, 15 Sept. 2004.

5. Malarek, *The Natashas*, p. 203.

6. *Sun*, 27 Jan. 2006.

7. Cler-Cunningham, *Violence Against Women,* p. 102.

8. REAL Women of Canada, "Prostitution in Canada and Other Countries", *REALity* (March/April 2005).

9. Pivot Legal Society, *Voices for Dignity*, p. 23.

10. De Vries, *Missing Sarah*, p. 102.

11. Highcrest, *At Home*, p. 126.

12. Stan Persky, *Mixed Media, Mixed Messages* (Vancouver: New Star Books, 1991), p. 50.

13. Cler-Cunningham, *Violence Against Women,* p. 5.

14. Pivot Legal Society, *Beyond Decriminalization: Sex Work, Human Rights and a New Framework for Law Reform* (Vancouver, 2006), p. 17.

15. Pivot Legal Society, *Voices for Dignity.*

Sources Consulted

Primary Documents:

VANCOUVER CITY ARCHIVES—
Board of Police Commissioners Records, Series 180-181
Fire Insurance Plan of Granville Townsite, August 1885, map 334
Police Department Records, Series 202, Prisoners' Record Books
Police Department Records, Series 209, Lennie Investigation Records
Mayor's Correspondence, Series 483
Vancouver Police Court, Series 192, Transcripts of Cases

NEWSPAPERS (SELECTED ISSUES)—
Vancouver Province
Vancouver Sun
Vancouver World, 1905-15

Books and Periodicals:

Acton, Janice, Penny Goldsmith and Bonnie Shepard, eds. *Women at Work: Ontario, 1850–1930*. Toronto: Women's Press, 1974.

Adachi, Ken. *The Enemy That Never Was: A History of the Japanese Canadians*. Toronto: McClelland and Stewart, 1991.

Aebi, Renata. "The Trafficking in Children for the Purpose of Prostitution: British Columbia, Canada". Paper prepared for the National Judicial Institute, International Instruments and Domestic Law Conference, Montreal, Nov. 9–12, 2001.

Anderson, Kay J. *Vancouver's Chinatown: Racial Discourse in Canada, 1875–1980*. Montreal: McGill-Queen's University Press, 1991.

Artibise, Alan F. J. *Winnipeg: A Social History of Urban Growth, 1874–1914*. Montreal: McGill-Queen's University Press, 1975.

Atkin, John. *Strathcona: Vancouver's First Neighbourhood*. Vancouver: Whitecap Books, 1994.

Backhouse, Constance. "Nineteenth-Century Canadian Prostitution Law: Reflection of a Discriminatory Society", *Social History*, vol. XVIII, no. 36 (Nov. 1985): 387–423.

_____. *Petticoats and Prejudice: Women and Law in Nineteenth-Century Canada*. Toronto: Women's Press, 1991.

Barman, Jean. *The Remarkable Adventures of Portuguese Joe Silvey*. Madeira Park, BC: Harbour Publishing, 2004.

_____. *Stanley Park's Secret: The Forgotten Families of Whoi Whoi, Kanaka Ranch and Brockton Point*. Madeira Park, BC: Harbour Publishing, 2005.

Bedford, Judy. "Prostitution in Calgary, 1905–14". *Alberta History*, vol. 29, no. 2 (Spring 1981): 1–11.

Bittle, Steven. *Youth Involvement in Prostitution: A Literature Review and Annotated Bibliography*. Ottawa: Dept. of Justice, Research and Statistics Division, April 2002.

British Columbia, Ministry of Attorney General. *Community Consultation on Prostitution in British Columbia: Overview of Results*. Victoria: Ministry of Attorney General, 1996.

British Columbia, Ministry of Attorney General. *Sexual Exploitation of Youth in British Columbia*. Victoria: Assistant Deputy Minister's Committee on Prostitution and the Sexual Exploitation of Youth, Ministry of Attorney General, 2000.

Brock, Deborah R. *Making Work, Making Trouble: Prostitution as a Social Problem*. Toronto: University of Toronto Press, 1998.

Buckley, Suzann, and Janice Dickin McGinnis. "Venereal Disease and Public Health Reform in Canada". *Canadian Historical Review*, vol. LXIII, no. 3 (Sept. 1982): 337–401.

Burk, Adrienne L. "A Politics of Visibility: Public Space, Monuments and Social Memory". PhD thesis, Simon Fraser University, 2003.

Campbell, Robert A. *Demon Rum or Easy Money: Government Control of Liquor in British Columbia from Prohibition to Privatization.* Ottawa: Carleton University Press, 1991.

_____. *Sit Down and Drink Your Beer: Regulating Vancouver's Beer Parlours, 1925–1954.* Toronto: University of Toronto Press, 2001.

Canning-Dew, Jo-Ann, ed., and Laurel Kimbley, comp. *Hastings and Main: Stories from an Inner City Neighbourhood.* Vancouver: New Star Books, 1987.

Cassel, Jay. *The Secret Plague: Venereal Disease in Canada 1838–1939.* Toronto: University of Toronto Press, 1987.

Chong, Denise. *The Concubine's Children.* Toronto: Penguin Canada, 1995.

Cler-Cunningham, Leonard, and Christine Christensen. *Violence Against Women in Vancouver's Street Level Sex Trade and the Police Response.* Vancouver: PACE Society, 2001.

Committee on Sexual Offences Against Children and Youths. *Sexual Offences Against Children in Canada.* 2 vols. Ottawa: Ministry of Supply and Services, 1984. [The Badgley Report]

Compton, Wayde, ed. *Bluesprint: Black British Columbian Literature and Orature.* Vancouver: Arsenal Pulp Press, 2001.

Currie, Sue. *Assessing the Violence Against Street-Involved Women in the Downtown Eastside/Strathcona Community.* Vancouver: Downtown Eastside Youth Activities Society, 1995.

Daum, Kimberly. *A Continuum of Abuse: Yesterday's Child Sex Abuse Victims are Today's Sexually Exploited Children are Tomorrow's Adult Sex Trade Workers.* Vancouver: Downtown Eastside Youth Activities Society, 1997.

_____. *A Cast of Contradictions.* Vancouver: Downtown Eastside Youth Activities Society, 1997.

De Vries, Maggie. *Missing Sarah: A Vancouver Woman Remembers Her Vanished Sister.* Toronto: Penguin Canada, 2003.

Doezema, Jo. "Loose Women or Lost Women? The re-emergence of the myth of 'white slavery' in contemporary discourses of 'trafficking in women". *Gender Issues*, vol. 18, no.1 (Winter 2000): 23–50. Accessed at *http://www.walnet.org/csis/papers/doezema-loose.html*.

Dubro, James. *Dragons of Crime: Inside the Asian Underworld*. Markham, Ont.: Octopus Publishing, 1992.

Eversole, Linda J. *Stella: Unrepentant Madam*. Victoria: Touchwood Editions, 2005.

Federal/Provincial/Territorial Working Group on Prostitution. *Report and Recommendations in respect of Legislation, Policy and Practices Concerning Prostitution-Related Activities*. Ottawa: Dept. of Justice, Dec. 1998.

Fingard, Judith. *The Dark Side of Life in Victorian Halifax*. Porters Lake, NS: Pottersfield Press, 1989.

Forbes, Corporal G.A. "Street Prostitution in Vancouver's West End". Report prepared for Vancouver Police Board and Vancouver City Council, Sept. 7, 1977.

Francis, Daniel. *L.D.: Mayor Louis Taylor and the Rise of Vancouver*. Vancouver: Arsenal Pulp Press, 2004.

Freund, Michaela. *The Politics of Naming: Constructing Prostitutes and Regulating Women in Vancouver, 1934–1945*. MA thesis, Simon Fraser University, 1995.

Gilfoyle, Timothy J. *City of Eros: New York City, Prostitution, and the Commercialization of Sex, 1790–1920*. New York: W.W. Norton & Co., 1992.

Glynn-Ward, Hilda. *The Writing on the Wall*. Toronto: University of Toronto Press, 1974. Originally published by Sun Publishing, 1921.

Grainger, M. Allerdale. *Woodsmen of the West*. Toronto: McClelland and Stewart, 1964. Originally published 1908.

Gray, James. *Red Lights on the Prairies*. Toronto: Macmillan of Canada, 1971.

Greene, Trevor. *Bad Date: The Lost Girls of Vancouver's Low Track*. Toronto: ECW Press, 2001.

Hagan, John, and Bill McCarthy. *Mean Streets: Youth Crime and Homelessness*. Cambridge: Cambridge University Press, 1998.

Hasson, Shlomo, and David Ley, eds. *Neighbourhood Organizations and the Welfare State*. Toronto: University of Toronto Press, 1994.

Highcrest, Alexandra. *At Home on the Stroll*. Toronto: Knopf Canada, 1997.

Hinther, Rhonda L. "The Oldest Profession in Winnipeg: The Culture of Prostitution in the Point Douglas Segregated District, 1909–1912". *Manitoba History*, no. 41 (Spring/Summer 2001): 2–13.

Johnston, Susan J. "Twice Slain: Female Sex-Trade Workers and Suicide in British Columbia, 1870–1920". *Journal of the Canadian Historical Association* (1994): 147–166.

Keller, Betty. *On the Shady Side: Vancouver 1886–1914*. Ganges, BC: Horsdal & Schubart, 1986.

Knight, Rolf. *Along the No. 20 Line: Reminiscences of the Vancouver Waterfront*. Vancouver: New Star Books, 1980.

Larsen, Nick. "Canadian Prostitution Control Between 1914 and 1970: An Exercise in Chauvinist Reasoning". *Canadian Journal of Law and Society*, vol. 7, no. 2 (Fall 1992): 137–156.

_____. "The Politics of Law Reform: Prostitution Policy in Canada, 1985–1995" in Nick Larsen and Brian Burtch, eds., *Law in Society: Canadian Readings*. Toronto: Harcourt Brace & Co., 1999: 60–74.

_____. "The Politics of Prostitution Control: Interest Group Politics in Four Canadian Cities". *International Journal of Urban and Regional Research*, vol. 16, no. 2 (June 1992): 169–189.

Lau, Evelyn. *Runaway: Diary of a Street Kid*. Toronto: HarperCollins, 1989.

_____. "The Shadow of Prostitution". *Inside Out: Reflections on a Life So Far*. Toronto: Doubleday Canada, 2001: 1–19.

Layton, Monique. *Prostitution in Vancouver (1973–1975): Official and Unofficial Reports*. Report submitted to the BC Police Commission, Sept. 1975.

Lowman, John. "Prostitution in Vancouver: Some Notes on the Genesis of a Social Problem". *Canadian Journal of Criminology*, vol. 28, no. 1 (Jan. 1986): 1–16.

_____. "Street Prostitution". In Vincent F. Sacco, ed., *Deviance: Conformity and Control in Canadian Society*. Scarborough, Ont.: Prentice-Hall Canada, 1992, pp. 49–94.

_____. *Street Prostitution: Assessing the Impact of the Law, Vancouver*. Ottawa: Dept. of Justice, 1989.

_____. "Submission to the Subcommittee on Solicitation Laws of the Standing Committee on Justice, Human Rights, Public Safety and Emergency Preparedness", Vancouver, 2005.

_____. "Vancouver Field Study of Prostitution". *Working Papers on Pornography and Prostitution, Report No. 8*. Ottawa: Dept. of Justice, 1984, 2 vols.

_____. "Violence and the Outlaw Status of (Street) Prostitution in Canada". *Violence Against Women*, vol. 6, no. 9 (Sept. 2000): 987–1011.

Lowman, John, M.A. Jackson, T.S. Palys and S. Gavigan, eds. *Regulating Sex: An Anthology of Commentaries on the Findings and Recommendations of the Badgley and Fraser Reports*. Vancouver: SFU School of Criminology, 1986.

MacInnes, Tom. *Oriental Occupation of British Columbia*. Vancouver: Sun Publishing, 1927.

Macdonald, Ian, and Betty O'Keefe. *The Mulligan Affair: Top Cop on the Make*. Surrey, BC: Heritage House, 1997.

McDonald, Robert A.J. *Making Vancouver: Class, Status and Social Boundaries, 1863-1913*. Vancouver: UBC Press, 1996.

McIntyre, Dr. Susan. "Strolling Away". Research report prepared for

Dept. of Justice. Ottawa, Aug. 2002.

McLaren, John. "Chasing the Social Evil: Moral Fervour and the Evolution of Canada's Prostitution Laws, 1867–1917". *Canadian Journal of Law and Society*, vol. 1 (1986): 125–65.

———. "White Slavers: The Reform of Canada's Prostitution Laws and Patterns of Enforcement, 1900–1920". *Criminal Justice History*, vol. 8 (1987): 53–121.

McLaren, John, and John Lowman. "Enforcing Canada's Prostitution Laws, 1892–1920: Rhetoric and Practice". In M.L. Friedland, ed., *Securing Compliance: Seven Case Studies*. Toronto: University of Toronto Press, 1990, pp. 21–87.

Mackie, John, and Sarah Reeder. *Vancouver: The Unknown City*. Vancouver: Arsenal Pulp Press, 2003.

Malarek, Victor. *The Natashas: The New Global Sex Trade*. Toronto: Viking Canada, 2003.

Marlatt, Daphne, and Carole Itter. *Opening Doors: Vancouver's East End*. Victoria: Ministry of Provincial Secretary and Government Services, Sound Heritage, 1979.

Marquis, Greg. "Vancouver Vice: The Police and the Negotiation of Morality, 1904–1935". In Hamar Foster and John McLaren, eds., *Essays in the History of Canadian Law, Vol VI: BC and the Yukon*. Toronto: University of Toronto Press, 1995: 242–273.

Matthews, Major J.S. *Early Vancouver: Narratives of Pioneers of Vancouver*. 2 vols. Vancouver: Brock Webler, 1932.

Moore, Vincent. *Angelo Branca: Gladiator of the Courts*. Vancouver: Douglas & McIntyre, 1981.

Moral and Social Reform Council of British Columbia. *Social Vice in Vancouver*. Vancouver, June 1912.

Morita, A. Katsuyoshi. *Powell Street Monogatari*. Burnaby, BC: Live Canada Publishing, 1988.

Nilsen, Deborah. "The 'Social Evil': Prostitution in Vancouver,

1900–1920". In Barbara Latham and Cathy Kess, eds., *In Her Own Right: Selected Essays on Women's History in British Columbia*. Victoria: Camosun College, 1980, pp. 205–227.

Persky, Stan. *The House That Jack Built: Mayor Jack Volrich and Vancouver Politics*. Vancouver: New Star Books, 1980.

_____. *Mixed Media, Mixed Messages*. Vancouver: New Star Books, 1991.

Pivot Legal Society. *Beyond Decriminalization: Sex Work, Human Rights and a New Framework for Law Reform*. Vancouver, 2006.

_____. *Voices for Dignity: A Call to End the Harms Caused by Canada's Sex Trade Laws*. Vancouver, 2005.

Potter, Greg, and Red Robinson. *Backstage Vancouver: A Century of Entertainment Legends*. Madeira Park, BC: Harbour Publishing, 2004.

REAL Women of Canada, "Prostitution in Canada and Other Countries". *REALity* (March/April 2005).

Robertson, Leslie, and Dara Culhane, eds. *In Plain Sight: Reflections on Life in Downtown Eastside Vancouver*. Vancouver: Talonbooks, 2005.

Roy, Patricia. *The Oriental Question: Consolidating the White Man's Province, 1914–41*. Vancouver: UBC Press, 2003.

Royal Commission on the Status of Women. *Report*. Ottawa: Information Canada, 1970.

Rule, Ann. *Green River, Running Red*. New York: Free Press, 2004.

Shier, Reid, ed. *Stan Douglas: Every Building on 100 West Hastings*. Vancouver: Contemporary Art Gallery/Arsenal Pulp Press, 2002.

Smith, Charleen P. *Regulating Prostitution in British Columbia, 1895–1930*. MA thesis, University of Calgary, 2001.

Sommers, Jeff. "Men at the Margin: Masculinity and Space in Downtown Vancouver, 1950–1986". *Urban Geography*, vol. 19, no. 4 (1998): 287–310.

Sommers, Jeff, and Nick Blomley. "'The worst block in Vancouver'". In Reid Shier, ed., *Stan Douglas: Every Building on 100 West Hastings*. Vancouver: Contemporary Art Gallery/Arsenal Pulp Press, 2002.

Special Committee on Pornography and Prostitution. *Pornography and Prostitution in Canada.* 2 vols. Ottawa: Dept. of Supply and Services, 1985. [The Fraser Report]

Strange, Carolyn. "From Modern Babylon to a City Upon a Hill: The Toronto Social Survey Commission of 1915 and the Search for Sexual Order in the City". In Roger Hall, William Westfall and Laurel Sefton MacDowell, eds., *Patterns of the Past: Interpreting Ontario's History.* Toronto: Dundurn Press, 1988, pp. 255–277.

Strange, Carolyn, and Tina Loo. *Making Good: Law and Moral Regulation in Canada, 1867–1939.* Toronto: University of Toronto Press, 1997.

Swan, Joe. *A Century of Service: The Vancouver Police 1886–1986.* Vancouver: Vancouver Police Historical Society, 1986.

Tong, Benson. *Unsubmissive Women: Chinese Prostitutes in Nineteenth-Century San Francisco.* Norman, OK: University of Oklahoma Press, 1994.

Trower, Peter. *Dead Man's Ticket.* Madeira Park, BC: Harbour Publishing, 1996.

Walkowitz, Judith R. *City of Dreadful Delight: Narratives of Sexual Danger in Late-Victorian London.* Chicago: University of Chicago Press, 1992.

Welsh, Robert M. *Sex, Vice and Morality: Tales from a Detective's Notebook.* Vancouver: self-published, 1994.

Williams, David Ricardo. *Mayor Gerry: The Remarkable Gerald Grattan McGeer.* Vancouver: Douglas & McIntyre, 1986.

Williams, Donald H. "The Suppression of Commercialized Prostitution in the City of Vancouver". *Journal of Social Hygiene,* vol. 27, no. 7 (Oct. 1941): 364–72.

Wilson, Ethel. *The Innocent Traveller.* Toronto: McClelland and Stewart, 1949.

Wilson, Robert. *The Wendy King Story.* Vancouver: Langen Communications, 1980.

Winterton, Chief D.L. "The Dilemma of Our Prostitution Laws".

Canadian Police Chief, vol. 69, no. 2 (April 1980): 5–6.

Wood, Daniel. "Missing". *Elm Street* (Nov. 1999): 96–110.

Yee, Paul. *Saltwater City: An Illustrated History of the Chinese in Vancouver*. Vancouver: Douglas & McIntyre, 1988.

Websites:

www.crimelibrary.com (an affiliate of the television network Court TV)

www.missingpeople.net (a site about Vancouver's Missing Women begun by Wayne Leng, a friend of Sarah de Vries, one of the women)

Index

191